communism

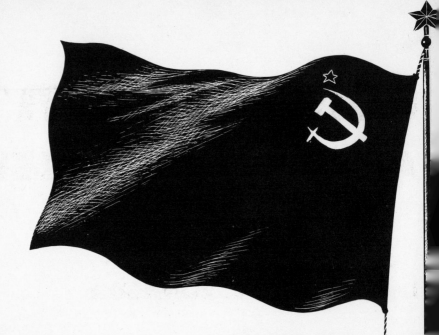

illustrated by

LEONARD EVERETT FISHER

communism
AN AMERICAN'S VIEW

by Gerald W. Johnson

WILLIAM MORROW & COMPANY
NEW YORK
1964

1547
5/7/64

CONTENTS

illustrations

communism

Chapter 1

The Roots of Communism

A hundred years ago there was a man in Germany named Karl Marx, who wrote so much and so well about Communism that a great many Americans think he invented it. He did not. There were Communists before Marx; and still earlier, before anyone had thought of calling them Communists, there were people who held the same kind of belief.

Karl Marx was a great man. Say that to the next American you happen to meet and the chances are more than even that he will be shocked, because that is not the light in which we have seen him. To most of us the name brings to mind some cartoonist's picture of a wild, bushy-haired creature with fierce whiskers, holding a bomb that he is about to throw. Marx in some ways was terrible, because he made some terrible mistakes. But he was a student such as the world has seldom seen. He read every book — that is, every serious book — he could put his hands on, and he not only read, he remembered what he read. More than that, when he dug up facts that most people had forgotten, or had never known, he could put them together and figure out what they meant.

That is a rare quality. It is so rare, indeed, that we have a special name for a man who can take a large number of facts, put them together, and from the whole collection bring out some important truth that nobody has seen before. We call him a philosopher.

Karl Marx was a philosopher, and a great one. He looked at the way the world was run in his time, and he saw much that he thought was wrong and much more that he thought was foolish.

All of us have wondered why things happen as they do — why one man works hard and gets richer and his neighbor works just as hard and gets poorer. But most of us stop with wondering. We decide that the problem is too hard, and give it up. Karl Marx never gave it up. Through a long life he kept studying, and he discovered a great deal. Some of

it has turned out to be wrong, but not all. Much that he discovered is true, and that is why wise people regard him as a great man.

Ask an American, "What is Communism?" and he will answer, correctly, "The kind of government they have in Russia and China."

When Karl Marx died there was no Communist government anywhere. At that time Communism was only a theory of what government ought to be — that is, government by the workers and for the workers. Marx believed that all governments then existing were governments of the workers, but for other people.

Marx had been dead more than thirty years when the Russians set up the first government planned according to his idea and therefore called Communist. But when they began to put Marx's rules into practice, they soon found that some of them wouldn't work in Russia. So they changed them, and the result is that the Russian government, the Union of Soviet Socialist Republics, is Marxist only in part; in some important respects it is strictly Russian.

Karl Marx was born and brought up in Germany, lived awhile in France, and finally settled down in England. Those were the countries he knew, and he planned a form of government that he thought would suit those countries. He knew little of Russia, but what he did know made him sure that his scheme would not fit that country, or any other that was backward — with many people unable to read or write, few factories, few railroads, highways, or canals, few engineers and scientists, few of all those things that go to make up what we call an "advanced" nation. As far as we know, Marx gave little thought to Russia, and he would have been astonished had he been told that Russia would be the first nation to try out his theories. He would have said that his scheme would certainly fail if it was tried in a backward country, and there is little doubt that it would have done so if the Russians had not changed it a great deal.

The result is that the American who wishes to understand what Communism means now must do more than study what Karl Marx wrote a hundred years ago. It is necessary to know what he thought, since that is the foundation of the whole scheme, but it is equally necessary to know how and why his ideas were changed by the men who built the Russian state.

To explain all Marx's ideas would require many books thicker than this one, but the basic notions on which he built all the rest of his argument are simple enough.

Marx noted, as many others had before him, that things become more valuable the more they are worked on. For instance, a log of wood, lying where it falls, is not much use to anyone. Cut into convenient lengths and split, it becomes firewood, which does have value because it can be used. If it is not cut, but sawed lengthwise, it becomes boards, which are more valuable than firewood. If the boards are smoothed, shaped, fitted together, stained, and varnished, they may become a table, many times more valuable than the rough boards. But the log becomes a table only after a great deal of work has been done upon it. Therefore, said Marx, the added value belongs by right to the men who did the work, because it is their labor that created the value.

Value meant to Marx, although his critics do

not often admit it, more than sales value. It meant also the satisfaction a man gets out of doing his job. This you cannot measure in money, or by any kind of yardstick. Marx counted this satisfaction as one of the values that the worker is entitled to get from his work. All around him Marx saw people making a living doing work in which they took no pleasure whatever, and he thought that was one of the worst of the things that were wrong with the world.

∨ When Marx was a young man living in Germany — from 1818, when he was born, to 1849, when he was driven out — a great deal of what was going on around him seemed to him foolish, and some of it downright wicked. Most people were poor, but some were rich. Many were so poor that they were hungry most of the time, but a few had so much wealth that they did not have to work at all. There were kings and princes and noblemen, and there were common people. The kings and nobility ruled, and the common people obeyed. It had always been so, and nothing could be done about it, or so the thoughtless supposed.

Marx could see no reason why such things should go on forever. He knew that workers were getting only a part of the value that labor added to raw material, and in his opinion it was an unfairly small part. Since it is work that adds value, people who do not work are not entitled to any of the added value, and there he went wrong. The man who supplies the tools with which the workman works has also contributed something. Marx admitted that work is impossible without tools and raw material on which to use them. The log must be there before the job can start; tools must be used on the wood before the log can be converted into a table. Raw materials and tools are just as necessary as labor, but they are not labor, they are capital.

Marx did not deny that part of the value added to raw material comes from the use of capital, but he asserted that the capital ought to belong to the people who do the work, not to others.

In the world as Marx saw it, practically all of the capital was owned by people who did little or none of the work, yet capital claimed, and was getting, more than its fair share of the added value. Marx did not hesitate to call this robbery and to call the capitalists who received it thieves. Naturally, this did not make him popular with factory owners, stockholders, bankers, and others who owned and dealt in capital.

No doubt some of these people knew that they held an unfair advantage and didn't care how unfair it was as long as they could hold on to it, which is to say they were no better than robbers. But the greater number were perfectly honest. They just couldn't see anything unfair in the system they were used to. If the king, for instance, had never done anything to deserve his riches, that was the way things were. Kings had always had riches, whether they had done anything to deserve them or not; it was the way the world was run, and anyone who objected was guilty of high treason.

Marx objected, so of course he soon got into trouble with the police. In the end he had to leave Prussia and finally went to London, where he spent the rest of his life.

Marx saw that under capitalism workers were being exploited, sometimes dreadfully exploited. He assumed, then, that under capitalism this would always be so, and the more power capital gained, the more it would exploit the workers. It never occurred to him, and it has only recently been realized by the more intelligent capitalists, that the time would come when exploiting labor would be unprofitable, because giving labor its fair share would pay better.

Marx believed that the time would come when exploitation would become so rough that labor could no longer endure it. Then the workers would band together, seize the means of production, and thereafter claim all the value that industrial processes add to raw material. This was Communism. It is based on at least one theory that time has shown to be very doubtful. That theory is that squeezing labor is the nature of capitalism, which cannot change its nature. If that were in fact true, then Marx was right in predicting a revolt. Since it seemed fairly certain that some owners would not give up their property without a fight, Communism to most people meant violence and bloodshed.

Marx, too, was aware of this possibility, but it did not disturb him much. He did not approve of violence but, perfectly sure that capitalism is bad by its very nature, he was equally sure that it was bound to get worse. By the time it became intolerable, Marx believed that few people would defend it, so the number that would have to be killed would be much too small to produce a great civil war. A little violence he was prepared to accept.

Yet, in the hundred years since Marx wrote, exactly the opposite has happened. The position of the workers in most strongly capitalistic countries has grown better, not worse. In the least capitalistic countries, such as Russia and China, Communism has been established at the cost of terrible civil wars and the loss of lives running into millions.

[It is a mistake to think that one can learn all about Communism by reading one book. But it is also a mistake to think that one must know everything about it in order to have a pretty good idea of what it is. The commonest mistake, though, is thinking that we know enough about it without reading anything. Some, indeed, go so far as to say that Americans ought not to study Communism for fear of having their minds upset and perhaps turning Communist. These people forget that when you don't understand what you are talking about you cannot form any intelligent opinion. It is foolish to try to oppose Communism, or to defend it, without any idea of where it is strong and where it is weak; and this we can learn fairly easily.

To understand something about Communism today, it is necessary to go back as far as 1917, the year of the Russian Revolution and the beginning of Communist government in Russia.

In 1917 there was a man named Ulyanov, but better known by his pen name, Vladimir Ilich Lenin, living in Switzerland. He was a Russian and had been for many years a student of the writings of Karl Marx. He used the pen name Lenin and he lived in Switzerland instead of Russia, because he was wanted by the Russian police for writing articles against the czar and the Russian government. Switzerland would hand over a man accused of robbery or murder, but not one accused of being against the government of another country.

Lenin's use of a pen name made it easy for the Swiss police to tell the Russians that they knew nobody named Ulyanov.

Lenin had personal as well as political reasons for hating the czarist government. When he was about seventeen, his older brother, then in his twenties, joined some other young men in a plot against the czar. But it seems that one among them was a spy, who betrayed the scheme to the police. They were arrested, and young Ulyanov was put to death. The younger boy never forgot or forgave. As soon as he was old enough he began stirring up trouble for the government. He was arrested and sent to Siberia, where he served for some years, but eventually got away and went to Switzerland. He had been living there for fourteen years when the First World War broke out.

This Lenin was a good thinker and a better writer. He became well known among radicals, that is, people who disliked the way the world was being managed and wanted to do something about it. The radicals, however, were only a small part of the whole population, and after war started, especially in 1917 when it had been raging for three years, nobody paid much attention to mere writers, radical or not. Yet this writer had studied the causes of the war and the way it was going to better effect than most of the statesmen and generals.

Germany and Great Britain had become rivals for world power, so naturally they disliked each other. Both were highly industrialized nations, needing raw materials for their factories, and both believed that the way to assure a supply of cheap raw materials was by holding as colonies the regions in which these materials were to be found. Inevitably, they got in each other's way, which added to the ill feeling. France was also an industrialized nation with a special grudge against Germany, by whom she had been beaten in 1870, losing the provinces of Alsace and Lorraine, which she wanted to get back. All the statesmen and generals understood these causes of the war and most of them looked no further; or if they did, they said nothing about it.

Lenin, however, understood all this and a great deal more. His study of Marx had convinced him that sometime the nationalistic system was bound to crack up. He thought also that nationalism was not strong enough to stand the strain of a great European war, in which he was nearly, but not quite, right. Thus it was easy for him to believe that the time for the crash of nationalism had come, and he looked for something to replace it.

Marx knew that as the people of the world change their habits of living and thinking, their systems of government must change. Everybody else who had studied history knew that. But Marx saw more clearly than most others that people's habits change faster than their systems of government. Thus the time must come to any system when it no longer fits the new ways and new conditions, and then the system must collapse. But as a rule the time comes before any except very alert people realize that it has arrived. Therefore, many will hold on to the old system when it is actually tottering to an inevitable fall.

Feeling certain in 1917 that nationalism could not survive the war, Lenin said so — in speeches, in newspaper and magazine articles, in pamphlets and books. Few people paid much attention to what he said, but among the few were certain government officials in Germany. They did not take the articles seriously, but they saw that they were so well written that they might confuse many people. No doubt they believed that Lenin was half crazy, but they also perceived that he was a first-rate troublemaker.

Now in 1917, after nearly three years of war, Russia was in a bad way. She had suffered tremendous defeats and terrible losses. The government of the czar was rotten. High officials were putting in their own pockets money intended to buy guns, ammunition, uniforms, and food for the armies, and they were sending the soldiers shells filled with sand instead of explosives, food too badly spoiled to be eaten, shoes made of pasteboard instead of good leather, and uniforms made of shoddy that quickly went to pieces.

Important jobs at home were given to men who couldn't handle them, and some men with hardly any brains at all were made generals. The Russian common soldiers were as brave and strong as any in the world, and many of their lower officers were first-rate, but the best soldiers in the world can't fight well with shells that will not explode, cannon that will burst, cartridges that will not fit their rifles, and food that cannot be eaten. It is no wonder that Russia was in a bad way.

This was fine for the Germans, and some German decided that it would be still finer if more trouble could be stirred up behind the lines, and Lenin was just the man to do it. So they gave him a railroad car, which they sealed up and put under guard, taking no chances of his getting loose in Germany, and carried him across the country, from Switzerland to the border of Finland. There they released him, knowing that he could easily get from Finland into Russia.

At the time it seemed a splendid idea, but it was perhaps the worst mistake the Germans made in the whole war, because it worked too well. Lenin created trouble right enough, but a great deal more than anyone had expected. The government of the czar had fallen before he reached Russia. Nicholas II had given up the throne, and a man named Kerensky had become the head of the state. He was a liberal, but not a radical.

He was also weak. He should have known that what the Russian people wanted was an end to the war at any price. Perhaps he did know it, but he lacked resolution enough to act on the knowledge. He let the British and French persuade him to make one more effort against the Germans. It ended in another terrible defeat, and with that the army went to pieces. The soldiers simply started home, and if their officers tried to stop them they shot the officers and went on.

This gave Lenin his chance. He had been busily organizing the radicals ever since his arrival. Lenin and his crowd seized the government. They called themselves Bolsheviks, which means

"majority," although they were not a majority but a very small part of the Russian people.

If this seems strange, there are two simple explanations of how it happened. First, the Bolsheviks knew exactly what they wanted to do, and how they meant to do it, while all the other factions were confused and uncertain. Second, the Bolshevik plan, on paper, looked reasonable. Indeed, as compared with czarism, it looked fine.

The scheme, roughly, was this: the country was to be divided into sixteen "republics," follow-

ing pretty closely the lines of the ancient provinces. These were to be subdivided into districts, villages, communes, and so on. In the smallest unit a committee (soviet) was to be formed representing the workers, soldiers, and peasants in that unit. This would be the local government, with authority to manage all strictly local affairs. The local soviet would elect representatives to the district, the district to the provincial, the provincial to the Supreme Soviet with authority over the whole Union. The Supreme Soviet would elect a central committee, which would be its executive committee. In theory, nowhere along the line could a nobleman, a banker, or a factory owner get in; only workers, soldiers, and peasants were to be represented. This was the system that Marx had called the Dictatorship of the Proletariat.

Since workers, soldiers, and peasants were by far the greater part of the Russian people the arrangement seemed to be fairly democratic, with power starting at the bottom and going up, step by step, to the Supreme Soviet and the central committee. It is still the main outline of the Russian system of government, although details are constantly being changed. Local soviets, districts, even republics have been merged, split up, sometimes abolished, and new ones set up in their place. This makes it risky to say that the government of Russia is exactly thus and so, because by the time the statement is printed it may have been changed. As this book was written the Supreme Soviet consisted of one hundred and seventy-five members, the central committee, now called the Presidium, of twenty-six. Yet in the opinion of most observers that statement should not be taken too seriously, even if the official figures are unchanged, for the Supreme Soviet invariably does whatever the Presidium suggests, and of the twenty-six members of the Presidium twenty are honorary officers without any real power. The ruling is done by not more than six men, chief of whom is the Secretary of the Communist party and Premier of the Union.

This is the scheme on paper; in actual practice power in Russia never has risen from the people up, it has gone from the Presidium down, and it has not gone down through the soviets, but through the Communist party.

In 1917 the Bolsheviks were the one group that was prepared, and it owed its readiness to the leadership of Lenin. Before he arrived in Russia, he had carefully worked out every step toward the seizure of power. We know that, because his ideas were published while the Russian Revolution was still in the future. He had written that it is impossible to stage a successful revolution unless you have first assembled a small group of bold, determined men who have agreed in advance on what each of them is to do and who can be relied on to do it.

The moment the revolution breaks out and the mobs begin to riot, these men must scatter, each leading a part of the crowd in a particular direction. Thus the government that is to be overthrown will find itself attacked on all sides at once, and will have to weaken its forces by dividing them.

These men, each assigned to a different task, but all taking orders from the same source, the central committee, were the Bolshevik party. They took their orders from the central committee because it alone had the whole plan in mind and knew where each man's work fitted, and the central committee was soon taking orders from Lenin, because he was the strongest man in the group, with probably the best brain and certainly the most carefully worked-out plan. When the central committee later became the Presidium, the leaders of the various units were the commissars. After the Revolution succeeded, the Bolsheviks, with all power in their hands, dropped that name and became the Communist party.

It may be that Lenin really intended, as soon as things settled down, to make the Communist party a party of all the Russian people instead of a relatively small group of men. We don't know, for things never settled down. Lenin believed, or came to believe, that they could never settle down as long as Russia was surrounded by capitalist nations, for he took Marx's word for it that capitalism is evil in its very nature, and therefore must be hostile to any government organized in another way. It is probable that this did not seem too important, for he confidently expected the whole system of nationalism to collapse soon.

When it failed to do so, it may be presumed

that he saw nothing for it but to continue to rely on his small group, and to allow nobody else to take an effective part in the government. So it has continued to this day.

The Communist party in Russia is not at all what Americans regard as a party. Anyone can join either of the two big American parties by registering as a Democrat or a Republican, but a Russian cannot join the Communist party without passing some severe tests. Today only about one Russian in twenty is a party member. Yet, since the Communist party alone is allowed to nominate candidates in an election, only party members really have a say in governing the country.

This confuses Americans. We are accustomed to think of three centers of political power — the administration and the two major parties. One party supports the administration, the other opposes it, but neither party is the administration, which is the government. In choosing his Cabinet the President is free to select men from either party. As this book was written, in the administration of President Kennedy, the Secretary of the Treasury and the Secretary of Defense, two very great officers of state, were chosen from the Republican party by a President who was a Democrat. In the legislative branch, when Congress is considering a bill that the President wishes to have passed, it frequently happens that some Democrats will vote against it and some Republicans for it. This could not happen in Russia where there is only one party, which controls the government at all times. ᗐAT Me, Boz

To us this seems the very opposite of democracy; it is the old system of government by aristocracy, the system against which we revolted in 1776. But Lenin would have denied, doubtless angrily, any such suggestion.

The chances are that what really influenced Lenin was a hangover from the old czarist theory — which at one time, be it remembered, had been the theory of all the rest of Europe — that to divide power is to destroy it. When the Constitution of the United States split the power of government three ways, into legislative, executive, and judicial branches, as wise a man as the English historian, Macaulay, predicted that the division would be the ruin of the republic.

In 1917 the fact that the American republic, instead of collapsing, had been steadily growing in power for a hundred and twenty-five years meant nothing to the Bolsheviks. They knew little about America, and most of what they believed was wrong. America was capitalistic. Marx had said that under capitalism the condition of the workers must steadily grow worse. It followed, therefore, that American workers must be slaves, and their belief that they were free proved only how easily they could be fooled, for Marx could not be wrong. Marx had said that all power must be kept in the hands of the workers. The Communist party represented the workers, the Presidium represented the party, and Lenin represented the Presidium. Therefore, all power was in the hands of the workers and Russia was a democracy.

Chapter 2

The Russian Revolution

When Lenin seized the government of Russia he took on a job so hard that most outsiders felt sure that it was impossible. Russia was beaten. The army had gone to pieces, and more than the army. In many parts of the country all law and order had gone to pieces, too. The peasants who worked on the great estates of the rich landlords had suffered terribly during the war. Few of them could read and write, and all of them were ignorant. They had a vague idea that somewhere there was a great man called the czar, who was the ruler of the whole country, but the only real authority they knew was the landlord, so it was natural for them to blame him for all their troubles. When ignorant men get a chance to get back at someone who, they feel, has been doing them wrong for many years, they are not likely to be nice about it. They were not nice in Russia.

All over the land the peasants began to form mobs. They had few weapons except pitchforks, scythes, and butcher knives, and no missiles except bricks and stones, but they were enough. In place after place they lynched the landlord and burned his house. Sometimes they murdered his whole family as well, and everywhere they seized the land that they had been working and said they were going to keep it, in spite of what anybody in the cities might say or do.

In the cities the workmen seized the factories in which they had been working, and if the owner objected they shot or hanged him. For a time it seemed that all civilization was about to disappear from Russia.

Lenin and his Bolsheviks held not much more than Petrograd, then the capital of Russia. (It was first named Saint Petersburg, in honor of the patron saint of Peter the Great, the czar who built the city; but during the war it was renamed Petrograd, because "Petersburg" was a German name, and afterward it became Leningrad, the name it bears today.) But the Bolsheviks, in spite of their name, were not a majority in Petrograd, much less in all Russia. Still they had to stop the Germans, hold down Kerensky's crowd, fight off the czar's crowd, and, most difficult of all, put a stop to the murdering, looting, and burning, bringing the country back under law and order again.

They stopped the Germans by the simple process of giving them whatever they demanded. At a town called Brest-Litovsk they signed a treaty handing over to the Germans all Poland and large slices of Russia itself. The treaty of Brest-Litovsk was one of the roughest imposed on a defeated nation in modern times. The Bolsheviks signed, but Lenin told the world they signed only because they had to. If a chance ever came to squirm out of that deal, he said frankly that he was going to do it. The chance came fairly soon, and he did do it.

But in solving one problem the Bolsheviks created another. The French and British were desperately afraid the German armies that had been fighting in Russia would now be turned against them as, in fact, they were. But turning great armies around, bringing them out of Russia and clear across Germany, and getting them ready to fight in a different kind of war took time. Before the eastern armies were ready to strike in the West, the French and British were already getting great quantities of supplies and a few men from the United States, brought into the war by the German policy of sinking our ships to prevent them from getting to Britain and France. The ships didn't matter so much, but the Germans could reach them only by submarines that torpedoed without warning, which meant killing or drowning our seamen. When the Germans did strike, the French and British, with some American help, managed to hold. The next year, with a great deal of American help, they broke the German power completely and brought about the peace of Versailles.

In early 1917, when the Russians quit the war, the French and British felt that the Bolsheviks had sold them out. Although they were too busy to do anything about it themselves, they cheerfully gave aid to anyone who was making trouble for the Bolsheviks. Of these, the most dangerous were those who wanted to bring the czar back to the throne, those who called themselves White

Russians, as opposed to the Red Russians, or Bolsheviks.

During the next three years five separate armies were organized by officers who had served under the czar, and Lenin's followers had to, and did, meet and defeat them all. It wasn't easy. The Western world, including the Americans, never has learned the full story of that war, because it was fought in great confusion and most of the records—when any were kept—were lost. But it was frightful. It was a civil war, Russian fighting against Russian, and, as Americans learned between 1861 and 1865, civil wars are often the bloodiest and fiercest kind. It is probable that Russia suffered more during this fighting than she had in the First World War, but most of the dreadful things that happened never became known to the outside world.

One atrocity, though, we did hear of. When Czar Nicholas gave up his throne, the Kerensky government allowed him and his family to occupy one of his palaces outside of Petrograd. But Petrograd was on the edge of Russia, and it was feared that one of the invading armies of White Russians might get close enough to liberate the czar, so the Bolsheviks removed the family to Ekaterinburg, far to the east. Later, however, a White Russian officer collected an army in Siberia and started westward. As it turned out, he was defeated before he reached Ekaterinburg, but he came uncomfortably close. Exactly what happened has never been known, because there are conflicting stories. The most likely seems to be that the commander in the place, responsible for keeping the czar, lost his head when the White Army approached. He must have realized what the Bolsheviks would do to him if he let Nicholas escape. Anyhow, he had the whole imperial family, including the czar, his wife, his young son, and his four daughters taken into the cellar of the house where they were living and shot to death.

This act horrified the people of the Western nations and made them more sure than ever that the Bolsheviks were inhuman monsters. But it has never been proved that Lenin ordered the deed, or even knew anything about it until it was all over.

Another thing that enraged the Westerners,

however, he certainly did do. In earlier years, before the First World War began, the British and French bankers and manufacturers had lent the Russians a great deal of money to help them build railroads, highways, and factories. This money Lenin refused to pay back. His argument was that they were not honest loans, that most of the money had been stolen by crooked officials, and that the lenders knew it would be stolen. It was a weak argument, and not many Westerners believed it was anything but a poor excuse for a dishonest course. They decided that the Bolsheviks were thieves as well as murderers, persons with whom it was impossible to deal in a civilized way. The United States, along with other nations, refused to recognize Lenin and his friends as the real government of Russia until they agreed to pay those debts. They would not agree, and Washington refused to recognize Russia for seventeen years.

Thus in making peace with Germany the Russians made bitter enemies of the Western nations, who, of course, refused to help the Bolshevik Communists with their domestic troubles. On the contrary, for a long time they did everything they could to multiply those troubles and make them worse. It is not surprising that the Russians thought this was plain malice, and to some extent it may have been just that; but the chief reason was that the West simply didn't understand the situation in Russia.

For that matter, the Russians themselves didn't understand it any too well, as is proved by the way they kept switching from one scheme to another, a practice they have kept up for nearly fifty years.

As far as outside events were concerned, the situation of Russia was not new. Nations had suffered terrible defeats before. Nations had gone through revolutions and civil wars before. Nations had seen their whole systems of law and order break down into confusion leading to anarchy, which is to say, no government. All this had happened to Russia, but none of it, or all of it put together, made her situation so different from all others.

The difference was that Russia, with certain habits of acting, and especially of thinking, suddenly found herself forced to deal with nations accustomed to quite different habits of acting, and especially of thinking. The same kind of thing, the collision of two cultures, has happened before, as, for instance, when the Goths sacked Rome and when the Moslems conquered Spain. In those cases, however, it was a matter of conqueror and conquered. It was not in this case. Russia had not conquered the West, or been conquered by it. It was a matter of adjustment between equals, and it was all the harder because neither side realized that there was much to adjust. Many Americans don't realize it yet. The best way to do that is to choose some particular clash between the two countries and study it.

Perhaps the most conspicuous clash is due to the Russian attitude toward religion. It is hostile, and in that particular the Russian Communists are following Marx, who called religion "the opium of the people," meaning that it drugged them into enduring what they would not endure if they were wide awake, just as a man who is drugged can endure a surgical operation because he doesn't feel the pain. This attitude has scandalized the West to such an extent that some Americans can hardly pronounce the word "Communism" by itself; they always make it "atheistic Communism."

It's true enough. The Communist leaders are always making violent attacks on religion. From our standpoint it is so silly that we cannot understand why men who in other respects seem to have brains can say such things.

Most Russians, including Lenin, had never regarded religion as something separate and apart from politics. They looked on the Church very much as they looked on the army and the police—as one of the tools used by the czar to maintain his power. So when they destroyed the other tools, and replaced them with tools of their own, they attacked the Church as fiercely as they had attacked the czar's army and police. They tried to replace Christianity with atheism, just as they had replaced the monarchy with Communism, and to this day they can't understand why, after nearly fifty years of effort, they have not succeeded.

But this is only part of the reason for the Communist hatred of religion. Another and perhaps more important part is that the Russians never went through the two experiences that convinced the people of the West, after many years and much quarreling and fighting, that religion and politics are separate and distinct, yet do not have to be hostile. It is the Russian belief that wherever two kinds of power exist, one must be supreme and the other inferior. This belief that power must be complete, total, or it will be nothing is the basis of the political doctrine called totalitarianism.

This delusion came straight down from the Byzantine Empire, from which the Russians drew their ideas of law and government, as the rest of Europe drew theirs from Rome. When Constantine the Great made Christianity the official religion of the Roman Empire, he did not divide his power; he simply made a Christian bishop the *pontifex maximus*, that is, the official in charge of religion, instead of a pagan *sacerdos*. When the Empire was divided, the bishop of Rome became the head religious official in the West and the patriarch of Constantinople became the head in the East, but both took orders from the emperor.

After some three centuries, though, the Roman Caesar fell; the Byzantine Caesar did not, for a thousand years and more. This released the bishop of Rome, the Pope, from servitude to any political ruler, for none of the European kings, not even Charlemagne, could restore the old authority of Caesar. But Russia, copying Byzantium, made the czar the supreme head of the Church. Centuries later, when the Bolsheviks revolted against the czar, they automatically, so to speak, revolted against the Church, for they regarded it as one of the agencies through which the czar maintained his power. They still clung to the idea that all power is the same, whether political or spiritual.

The people of the West thought so, too, for centuries. What made them abandon that opinion was, first, the Renaissance, and later, the Reformation. The Renaissance taught the people in those nations that had been part of the Roman Empire that it is important to know the truth about this world as well as about heaven and life after death. In the Dark Ages it had been believed that learning and art were useful only to religion, therefore such things were left almost entirely to priests and monks. It was the Renaissance that set great numbers of laymen to studying the world around them, and after a long time that study led to modern science.

The Reformation had a different, but quite as important effect. It finally destroyed in the West the belief that the political power has authority over the spiritual. This separation of power came to be the accepted doctrine of the whole West, Catholic and Protestant, although Protestants put added emphasis upon the parallel doctrine that the spiritual power has no authority over the political.

Remember, though, that this change in Western ways of thinking and acting was not made quickly or easily. Many bitter years, filled with turmoil and bloodshed, passed before it was established. Some of the most savage wars in history were fought to bring it about, and many great crimes were committed in the vain effort to prevent it. John Huss and Giordano Bruno were burned at the stake, and Girolamo Savonarola hanged for daring to think for themselves. Galileo was forced to say that he had lied, when he knew that he had told the truth about the sun and the stars. Eventually, though, it was done. Long before 1917, in all the nations that had belonged to the old Roman Empire, most people believed that freedom to act and, even more, freedom to think are good things, although it had to be admitted that some people still lacked both.

But Russia had hardly been touched by the Renaissance and not at all by the Reformation. Russia bordered on the Byzantine Empire, and as the country slowly came out of barbarism it took its ideas and ideals from Byzantium, where the idea of freedom of the mind as the foundation of all other liberty had never existed. So it did not penetrate Russia, except through a few great writers and thinkers; and when they tried to speak or write of freedom they were quickly silenced or even put to death, as in the case of Lenin's older brother.

Religion is only a sample, so to speak, of the many wide differences between the way Russians thought and the way Americans and most Europeans thought in 1917. These differences account for the curious fact that then nobody understood how the Bolsheviks could take over and hold such a vast country as Russia. They couldn't have done it in any Western nation. They tried in various places, in Germany, in Italy, in Spain, even in France and England. But in France and England, the most democratic countries in Europe, they were stopped before they really got started, and in Germany, Italy, and Spain all they did was to provoke a violent reaction that led to the rise of dictators who were worse than Communists in Germany and Italy, and nearly as bad in Spain. When it came to bloody tyranny, Hitler in Germany and Mussolini in Italy could have given lessons to Lenin.

The chief reason for Bolshevik success in Russia was that their leader knew exactly what he wanted, and, knowing Russia, knew exactly how to get it, while no other faction had such a man. Lenin had a carefully worked-out plan, so he drove straight ahead. In a short time he had not only seized the government, but had also compelled other factions to follow his lead or get out. Thus the Bolsheviks became the whole Russian Communist party. After that, there was no point in calling them Bolsheviks. They were the Communists, all the Communists, and the only Communists in Russia.

Lenin's political doctrine that had been straight Marxism now became Marxism-Leninism in Russia. That is how Communism in Russia became not what Marx said, but what Lenin said that Marx meant, which is not necessarily the same thing.

This makes it necessary to consider what kind of man Lenin was, and it is not easy to describe him. There is no doubt that he was remarkable in many ways, and in some ways he was great, but he was certainly very dangerous.

Lenin had a splendid mind and great energy, but he was hard all the way through. He had the one quality that can harden a man not only outside, but right through to the center. We call it moral certainty, which means that the man who has it is not merely sure that he is right, but also sure that he can't go wrong. Such men are always dangerous.

What makes moral certainty dangerous is the fact that when a man is convinced that he can't go wrong, it follows that whatever he does is bound to be right, however it may look to outsiders. He accepts for truth what is perhaps the biggest lie ever told — the lie that if you mean well anything you do to achieve your purpose is proper. When a man has swallowed that lie, he can do horrible things with a clear conscience.

Nearly all of us have a touch of this quality, but fortunately most people are morally certain only a small part of the time. It is seldom that a man with a really powerful mind is so afflicted, but when it does happen the damage he can do is without limit.

Vladimir Ilich Lenin, with a keen mind, vast learning, and tremendous energy, did not hesitate to say that it is all right to lie, steal, betray, and even murder, if you do it, not for your own profit, but for the good of mankind.

Westerners who read that sort of thing for the first time often find themselves in a sort of daze. They just can't see how a man could say such things, certainly not a man as able and learned as this one.

What they forget is that it isn't so long ago — not long as measured by history — that their own ancestors thought the same way. During the last four centuries ancestors of modern Europeans, and therefore of most Americans, fought and suffered and died to do away with that idea and to replace it with the principle that every man is responsible for his own acts.

But a man can't be held responsible for acting in one way unless he is free to act in another way. There must be freedom of the mind before there can be freedom of action. But how can a man learn if nobody is allowed to teach him, and how can anybody teach if he is not allowed to explain what he thinks? There must be freedom of speech if there is to be any freedom of the mind.

This truth, which our ancestors learned painfully, has now become so much a part of what everybody thinks that we do not know that we know it, until some extraordinary event startles us into thinking about it.

But Lenin was a Russian, and the Russians, having missed both the Renaissance and the Reformation, did not have bred in their bones as high a respect for the value of liberty as the Westerners have. In this respect, Lenin's thought was just four hundred years behind Western thought.

Many Americans have never realized this. It seems to them that Communism is not only completely new, but wicked with a kind of wickedness never seen in the world before. That is one reason why they are so afraid of it. They would not like it any better, but it would scare them less, if they could realize that Communist scorn of what we regard as morality is nothing new, but a kind of thinking that the Western nations have outgrown.

Up to this point we have been speaking of Lenin as if he had been the whole Communist party in Russia. He was not. He had many assistants, some of them men with first-rate minds and one, in particular, so brilliant that he was almost the equal of Lenin himself. Yet at the time this book was written and for many years before, this man's name was never mentioned in Moscow, and every effort was put forth to make the Russian people forget that he ever existed. But the rest of the world remembers him with good reason. His name was Leon Trotsky, and he was the other half of the team of Lenin and Trotsky that made a nation of Soviet Russia.

They worked well together because each had something that the other lacked. Just where one was weak the other was strong. Both were bookish men, but Lenin more so. Both were active men, but Trotsky more so. Both were hard, determined men, but Lenin learned more about history, Trotsky more about people. Before 1917 Lenin had spent most of his life in libraries, Trotsky most of his — except when he was in jail, dodging the police, or being sent to and escaping from Siberia — on the streets and in offices where he mingled with all sorts of people. Among other things he had been for some years a newspaper reporter in Vienna.

They were both in Russia in 1917. After the Germans had been appeased at Brest-Litovsk and had started wheeling their armies around toward France, the next big job was to stop the White Russians from marching in and putting the czar back on the throne. Trotsky was the man who did it. Later this was denied flatly, and for thirty years the official story was that he had nothing to do with it. But the official story was a lie made up to help erase the memory of Leon Trotsky from Russian minds.

What Trotsky did was a feat seldom matched in history. There was no longer a Russian army. Some of its regiments held together and followed the White Russian generals, but not many. Most simply dissolved. By far the greater number of the soldiers who had formed the Russian army were wandering around the country in small bands, not knowing which way to turn, and living by robbing the country people wherever they could find food. Trotsky's job was to get these men together, form them into armies, give them weapons, and — most important and hardest of all — persuade them to fight.

This job he did. How, nobody ever knew, perhaps not even Trotsky. But he was a superb orator, and one of the best organizers ever known. Wherever he found a group of wandering soldiers he made them a speech so eloquent that by the time he was through they were fired with enthusiasm and ready to fight anybody they were told was an enemy of Russia. Somehow, somewhere, he found

guns and ammunition, and somehow, somewhere, he scraped together enough food to keep his men alive. It took the better part of three years, but at last all five White Armies were defeated and the civil war was won.

After three frightful years the danger that a new czar would be put on the throne was over. Then came the task of rebuilding all that the wars had destroyed, which was very nearly everything in Russia except the land itself. It was such a tremendous task that it had not been completed twenty years later, when the Second World War burst upon Russia, after which most of the job had to be done all over again. But the way Lenin and Trotsky went about it is the story of how modern Communism came into existence.

Chapter 3

Lenin

Ask anyone what was the most important thing Lenin and Trotsky did, and he will answer that they made Russia Communist. But some people are not sure that it is the right answer, because they did another thing that in the end may be more important—they made Communism Russian.

Some reader may ask, what's the difference, as far as we are concerned? The difference is that if Communism has been made Russian our difficulties are increased, for it has been made harder for us to understand.

If it is true that what we are having to deal with today is not so much Communism as Russianism— the scholarly term is Slavism, as the Russians are Slavs—not so much the ideas of Marx as those of Lenin and the men who followed him—it is no wonder that we are puzzled, for few of us know what is behind those ideas. We have discovered that such a word as democracy, for example, means one thing when the President of the United States uses it, and something quite different when a Russian dictator uses it. So when the Russian asserts that he believes in democracy, it is natural for us to jump to the conclusion that he is a liar and the truth is not in him.

But suppose the word actually means to the Russian something different from what it means to the American? Don't think that it is impossible, for it may mean different things to the American, depending upon the way it is used. Democracy may mean a political party, as opposed to the Republican party. It may mean a system of government, as opposed to monarchy. Or it may mean a whole social system, as opposed to aristocracy. It is therefore not impossible that in the mind of the Russian it may have a fourth meaning about which we know nothing. The man may think quite sincerely that he is telling the truth, and a man who intends to tell the truth may be mistaken, but he is not a liar.

The three great revolutions in modern times, the American, beginning in 1776, the French, beginning in 1789, and the Russian, beginning in 1917, had the same object, namely, to make it possible for all men, not merely a few, to enjoy freedom and justice, or at least more freedom and justice than they had enjoyed under the old government. But only one of the three was carried through by the same people that started it. That was the American, and it was the only one of the three that did what it started out to do, at least in part.

Nobody can claim that the Americans won perfect freedom and perfect justice for all the people of this country, but at least they made a start. At the end of the fighting the American people certainly had more freedom, and most of us believe that they had a better chance to obtain justice than they had had under the British king.

Some historians declare that ours was not a real revolution, only a civil war, or at most half a revolution, in which one party replaced another without any deep change in system. Yet in America monarchy was overthrown. Legal recognition of

classes—nobility, gentry, commoners—was overthrown. The right of the eldest son to inherit his
father's whole estate was overthrown. The Church
was separated from the state. Entail, a device by
which great estates passed from generation to generation without being broken up, was abolished.
It was formally proclaimed as one of the basic
principles of government that in the eyes of the
law, if nowhere else, "all men are created equal
and endowed by their Creator with inalienable
rights." If all this didn't constitute a deep change
in the social system, what would?

Then comes the question, why didn't the others
do as well? The reason is that in America at the
time of the Revolution everybody, or nearly everybody, had enough to eat. Most Americans then
were poor, but there is a vast difference between
being poor and being in desperate want. In 1776
this country was rural. The largest city, Philadel-
phia, had about 25,000 people, and Boston, New
York, and Baltimore were little more than large
villages. Washington was a forest, Chicago a
swamp, Detroit a trading post in the woods, Los
Angeles a fishing village. The vast majority of

Americans lived on farms that they owned and cultivated as they saw fit, and of course they saw fit to raise enough food, simple but ample. It was almost unheard of for anyone to live in real want, hungry from year's end to year's end.

In Paris, when the king's government fell, thousands of creatures so hungry, so ill-clad, so ill-housed that they seemed hardly human came swarming out of the slums. Their condition was indicated by the name given them; they were the sansculottes, a word that meant "no breeches."

Under the king the sansculottes had been held down rigidly by the police, aided when necessary by the army. If they dared show themselves near the royal palace or the great houses of the nobility, they were handled roughly and quickly hustled back to their wretched dens, so the fine ladies and gentlemen, seldom seeing them, hardly knew that they existed. But as soon as the revolt began they surged out. They formed the mob that stormed the hated prison, the Bastille. They manned the barricades thrown up in the streets to prevent the king's troops from stamping out the Revolution. They rushed into the galleries when the National

Assembly met, and put the delegates in fear of their lives.

Somehow they had to be taken care of, and that at the very moment when all the remaining kings of Europe were sending their armies against France. It was a desperate moment, calling for desperate efforts. In the stress and strain the original objects of the Revolution, freedom and justice, were pushed aside, leadership came into the hands of more and more desperate men, while moderates went to death or into exile. In the end the tough young artillery officer, Napoleon Bonaparte, blasted the sansculottes off the streets with grapeshot, and soon took over the whole show himself. Such things as freedom and justice interested him very little, but power interested him very much and in the end he had it all.

Something similar happened in Russia a century and a quarter later, with the difference that in Russia a large part of the country was starving, not merely the people of the city slums. When Lenin seized the government in 1917, he put himself in charge of a country in which millions of people were without food. Any ruler who faces that kind of situation has one duty that comes ahead of everything else. It is the duty of feeding the people. If that is not done, soon the ruler will have, in theory, nobody left to rule. In fact, not theory, however, the people will form mobs that will tear everything to pieces, probably including the ruler, as they did in the French Revolution.

However, Russia is a very large country and the wars had not completely covered it. In some sections there was a surplus of food. But with railroads torn up, highway bridges broken down, no money that anyone wanted to accept, and robber bands of former soldiers wandering about, there was no way of moving the food from where it was grown to where it was needed.

As fast as Trotsky organized the deserters into units that would obey orders, Lenin sent them to places where there was food and took it. If the owner agreed, he was given paper money issued by the new government. If he refused, he was killed and the food taken anyhow. This was neither freedom nor justice, nor did it pretend to be. It was war, which is, as Lenin well knew, the sum of everything evil.

More than that, it was the worst kind of war because the armies marching toward Moscow, to which the Communists had moved the government from Petrograd, were not the more or less civilized armies of the kings of Europe. They were collections of rabble that the various White Russian generals had managed to scrape together. They included some honest and patriotic men, but they also included many of the worst scoundrels in Russia. Wherever they went they robbed, abused, and often killed the peasants, including women and children. Trotsky's Red Armies were kept under better control, but even they took no prisoners. Every White Russian who fell into their hands was immediately killed, as were all the Reds that the Whites captured. But the only peasants the Reds murdered were those who tried to hold back something that the Reds needed, and they did not make a practice of abusing women and children. So the country people came to think of them as somewhat better than the Whites, and became willing to help them, which meant that the Whites had lost the civil war.

But it also meant that Lenin and those around

him held all the power firmly in their own hands, and held it as by right, not by consent of the soviets. They called their new government the Union of Soviet Socialist Republics, but the local soviets, supposed to be the foundation of the whole structure, were reduced to little more than neighborhood councils. They could decide to build a new culvert and which local road should be repaired first, but in larger affairs they were much less powerful than the Board of County Commissioners in an American State. The district and regional soviets also simply carried out the orders sent down from Moscow.

The Russian Revolution had gone the way the French Revolution had gone, into dictatorship.

Lenin's model was Karl Marx who had been, like Lenin, a thinker, not a fighter, and the government Lenin imposed upon Russia was built on the pattern dreamed up by Marx. Agreement in thought was what Marx demanded first of all, and so did his disciple, Lenin. It was the minds rather than the bodies of men that both sought to dominate.

No other great state had ever been built on this

pattern, which is one reason why it has so frightened the rest of the world. Tyrants of many kinds —kings, conquerors, emperors, dictators—the world has long known, and it has slowly learned how to deal with them, for they all followed pretty much the same line, which led to failure in the end. Even as great a dictator as Napoleon didn't last long. But Lenin was trying something that had never been tried before, so the world did not have the same assurance that he was bound to fail. A great many Westerners were terrified by him, not because they were sure that he was wrong, but because they feared that he might be right.

In fact, he was right to the extent that the dictators before him had been right. People, Russians or any other, prefer a tyrant to no government at all; for while a tyrant is dangerous to anyone who angers him, with no government there is no safety anywhere. A tyrant may rob and oppress his people, but he will not allow anyone else to do so, and it is better to be robbed and oppressed by one man than by every gang of armed men that comes along. For years before Lenin restored order the Russian common people had been the victims of roving bands of cutthroats and the White Armies, which were little if any better. The new government put a stop to that. Of course the people liked it.

For many generations the government of the Russian czars had been the worst in Europe, unless that of the Turkish sultans was equally bad. The Russian people, especially the country people, were used to being ordered about by some higher-up. Indeed, until 1861 the peasants had been serfs, and a serf is so close to a slave that it takes a great many words to explain the difference. Serfs were not put up on the auction block and sold one by one as slaves were; but if a man bought an estate, the serfs working on the land went with it, and if they ran away officers of the law would arrest them and bring them back. The liberal Czar Alexander II did away with that system, but he did it because he chose to, not because any parliament or congress or other lawmaking body compelled him, for nobody could compel the czar. He was what is called an absolute monarch, the only one left in Europe.

A small number of Russians, well-educated people who had traveled abroad, or at least had read foreign books and newspapers, knew that the rest of Europe had long ago done away with absolute monarchy and wished to see their own country do so. But the high nobility around the czar and some of the rich businessmen and landowners were quite satisfied with absolutism, because they were making a good thing out of it, and these men made life hard for anyone bold enough to say publicly that Russia ought to have a better system.

As time went on, more and more people learned how bad their government really was. In part, they were taught by the great Russian writers—novelists, poets, and playwrights—who had grasped the idea of political liberty; and in part by political thinkers such as Kropotkin, who, although born a prince and in boyhood a page to the czar, became convinced by Marx before Lenin was, and has some claim to be regarded as the first great Russian Communist. But the more such people's ideas spread, the tougher the government became. Lenin's older brother was only one of a dreadfully large number of people who were put to death for demanding freedom, and for every one executed at least ten others were sent to the bleak wastes of Siberia as exiles.

In order to find out who was talking against it, the government employed large numbers of spies —the dreaded secret police who went about in plain clothes listening to what their neighbors said and reporting them to the uniformed police. It got so that a man dared not criticize the government even to his own brother, for fear the brother might be a member of the secret police. This went on so long that ignorant people—and a great many Russians, especially among the peasants, could neither read nor write—had become accustomed to it and supposed that a government couldn't be run in any other way.

This was the state of affairs when Lenin came to power. The first of the Communist dictators was probably right in thinking that in the special case of Russia it was possible to rule a great country from the top down.

Lenin was certainly a severe dictator. He constantly used the hangman's rope and the firing squad to get rid of his enemies, but it must be admitted that he usually took some pains to make sure that they were, in fact, enemies before he killed them. He did not make a practice of having men shot or hanged on mere suspicion, or out of fear that they might become enemies.

Thus while it cannot be denied that he was rough, it was only outside of Russia that he was looked on as a monster. Highly intelligent Russians might admit that at times he went too far, but they could not forget that without Lenin there probably would have been no Russia by 1925. At best it would have been split into a number of small nations. At worst, it would have been divided among Poland, Germany, Czechoslovakia, Rumania, and others. Perhaps even Finland might have taken Petrograd. It was largely due to Lenin that it escaped this peril, and people remembered that.

Lenin did another thing more important than bringing the country through the wars. He gave the great masses of the Russians hope. In American eyes Lenin's promise to them was a delusion, so plainly a fake that we cannot understand how

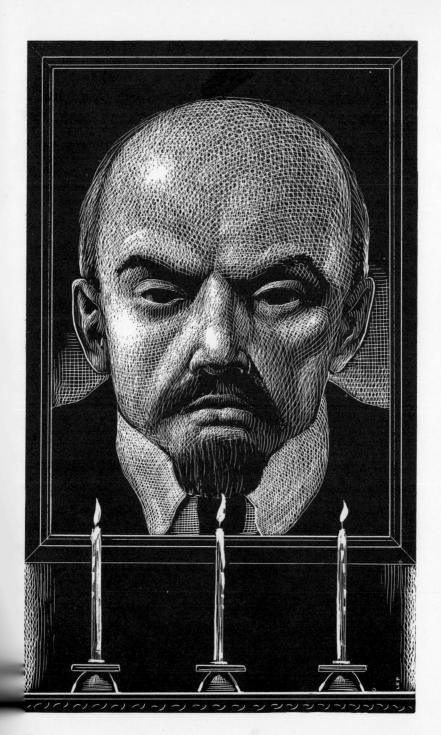

anyone could be taken in by it. We forget that up to Lenin's time almost nobody among the powerful had taken the trouble to give the poorest of the Russians anything except kicks and curses and beatings if he didn't do his work properly. Czar Alexander II did free the serfs, but they were not much better off than they had been before, because he did nothing effective to enable them to hold the land they worked.

Now came Lenin promising the destitute to divide the wealth of Russia equally among all the people. To them it seemed a glorious promise. They were too ignorant to realize that after the wars there was little left in Russia and that if it had been divided equally all would have been equally poor. What the peasants and the poorer factory workers saw, and all that they saw, was a promised end to the misery they and their forefathers had endured for hundreds of years, and it was to come through Lenin. It is no wonder that all over Russia they burned candles before his picture and worshiped him like a god.

More than that—this is a truth that we Americans hate to admit, but we might as well face it—

before he died Lenin began to make good. He couldn't perform miracles. No more than any other man could he create out of nothing food and clothing and railroads and highways and machinery and all the other things that Russia needed. But he did away with the oppressive laws that made every peasant's son a peasant all his life. He did away with grand dukes and princes and other kinds of noblemen, and with the great landlords— many he did away with quite literally by killing them, and the rest he drove out of the country. He made plans to organize the government according to the rules drawn up by Karl Marx, and by the time he died if the common people were still pretty miserable, they were better off than they had been and—most important of all—they had hope of being better off in the future.

Some Americans, seeing that most Russians lack a great many things we would be unhappy without, think that the Russians must also be unhappy and will presently rise up against their government. They forget that the fact that a man is in bad shape today is not proof that he is miserable. If he was in worse shape yesterday and feels sure that he is going to be in better shape tomorrow, he is likely to be quite cheerful. Tatters do not prove misery. If a Russian had, like the sans-culottes, no breeches yesterday, and has only a ragged pair today, but thinks he has an excellent chance of getting a whole new suit tomorrow, he is unlikely to be in a mood to upset everything.

That seems to explain two things: first, why that very hard character, Lenin, is worshiped by Russians as Americans never worshiped George Washington; and second, why Communism has lasted nearly fifty years without being overthrown by the Russian people.

Lenin moved the government from Petrograd, dangerously near the edge of Russia, back to the old capital, Moscow, in the heart of the country and not to be reached by any foreign army except by a long and difficult march. In Moscow he set up his headquarters in the Kremlin, a section of the city containing the czar's palace, many government buildings, and several churches, all surrounded by a high and very strong wall, for the czars never had much confidence in the loyalty of their people.

Neither had the Communists. All important government business was planned inside the Kremlin, with the people shut out. Managing a large country is a tremendous job, so there must have been endless arguing and debating among the chief Communists. We know, for instance, that Trotsky did not approve of all Lenin's ideas,

and said so, yet without losing Lenin's confidence. For the most part, though, all disagreements were kept behind that wall, and the rest of the world knew nothing about them. When a certain course of action had been decided by the chiefs, the people were told how it was to be, and that was that.

We do know, however, that once the fighting had been ended and it was time to organize the country for peace, Lenin found that many of Marx's ideas simply would not work. It is easy to see why. Marx was born and brought up in a country that was being highly industrialized. Even a hundred years ago Germany had many factories, enormous quantities of machinery, a fine railroad system, and good highways everywhere. So had France and England.

But Russia had little of any of these things. This meant that in Germany you could easily do things that simply couldn't be done in Russia. The greatest advantage that the highly industrialized countries had, however, was not the equipment, but the men who could run the equipment, keep it in repair, and improve it—mechanics, engineers, inventors, scientists. Even more important were the research men, that is, men who were constantly finding out things that had not been known before, new knowledge that would enable them to build better machines, plan new processes, and make use of materials that had never been used before.

All the highly industrialized countries had many such men, Russia almost none; and without them a great many Marxist ideas couldn't be made to work. Marx knew this very well; he always said that Communism would come first in the advanced countries and later in backward countries, such as Russia then was.

We know that Lenin discovered this because in 1921 he proclaimed what he called the New Economic Policy. The name was a cover-up, for the scheme was certainly not a new policy but a return, meant to be temporary, to the way that had been followed before in doing certain kinds of business. The peasants, in particular, were to be allowed to work as they had always worked, raising their crops as they saw fit and selling them for what they could get. Some merchants, too, were to be allowed to sell some kinds of goods freely, and even in the factories a good workman was to be paid more than a bad one.

This was a retreat from pure Communism and Lenin knew it, but it had to be done to prevent a collapse. The curious thing is that it was a retreat from the most advanced capitalism as well. The capitalism of the United States is as advanced as any in the world, and under it we have found that dividing the land into small farms, each worked by one man, is not sound agricultural economics. The way to produce on a given number of acres the largest possible quantity of any farm product is to plow, plant, and harvest with power-driven machines—tractors, combines, and so on. But machines are expensive and will not pay for themselves unless they are used to cultivate a great many acres.

For this reason the small farm has been rapidly disappearing in America, and more and more of our farm products are grown on large estates where costly machines can be used profitably. Without knowing it, we have been introducing something very like the "collectivized" farm system that Lenin had planned for Russia. Here, now, is an interesting fact that nearly all Americans overlook: under Lenin the collectivized farm was such a complete failure that he had to back away from it with the New Economic Policy, and although since Lenin it has been brought back, it has never worked well. Yet with us, it *has* worked well, though with some drawbacks.

After Lenin, when collectivized farming was established in Russia, it was not set up by the farmers themselves, but by law.

If an American farmer is faced with the choice of sitting on his forty acres and living half-starved, or going into town and making good money, he is, you might say, forced to go. But there is a difference between being forced in that way, and being forced by a soldier behind you, prodding you with a bayonet. Furthermore, when an American farmer did move, he moved in any direction he pleased; the Russian peasant who was no longer needed on the farm was often loaded on a train and taken someplace, perhaps a thousand miles from his old home, where the government needed hands.

Slave labor may be as good as free labor in building a pyramid, but not in anything where the will to work has an important effect on the product. Lenin discovered this and, being a realist, he backed away from the collective farm system just at the moment when Americans, applying it in a different way, were making a success of it. Hopeful Americans promptly jumped to the conclusion that he was backing away from Communism. It never occurred to them that what he was actually backing away from was a form of capitalism too advanced to be put to work in Russia.

Lenin, of course, was the first dictator in Russia with absolute power. Most Western statesmen, knowing that their own countries would revolt against absolutism, thought that Russia, too, would do so. For many years they felt sure that Communism would soon blow up from within, because it was an impossible system. Even today, when Russian Communism has lasted nearly fifty years and has spread through China, there are Americans who still argue that it is bound to collapse because of its basic weakness. To prove it, they point out that no Western nation has yet adopted Communism of its own choice. It has been forced upon some, such as Poland, Hungary, and Czechoslovakia, but only through fraudulent elections backed by the Red Army.

This is literally true. But the trouble with that argument is that it is often used as an excuse for not giving Communism enough careful study to reveal its points of strength. This might do no great harm if the thing were certain to collapse soon; but it hasn't collapsed, and to know why is highly important. The danger of Communism to us lies, not in its weakness, but in its strength, which means that we ought to know more about where it is strong than where it is weak.

This much is certain: a system that has lasted nearly fifty years didn't blow up "soon," as most of us understand the word. A system that stood up under the shock of a Second World War more furious than the First can't have any fatal internal weakness. A system that has taken over a nation of six hundred million people, China, is not impossible. A system that has taken over territory,

Cuba, in close contact with the United States, must have been able to show those people a picture of itself that is not the nightmare we see in Communism.

Communism is not bad because it is weak, for it is very strong. It is not bad because Communists are enemies of the human race, because to one third of the human race Communists are their only friends. It is not bad because it holds that factories, farms, and many other kinds of property ought to belong to the state, not to private persons; other countries have at one time or another tried out this idea.

Communism has plenty of minor faults, but the great one, the fatal one, is that it denies to the common man the one kind of freedom that makes all the other kinds worthwhile. That is freedom of the mind.

The nations in which Communism has been stopped all accept the principle that the common man ought to be free to think for himself and to say what he thinks. The nations through which Communism has spread are all nations in which for centuries it has been extremely dangerous, often fatal, for the common man to think for himself and say what he thinks.

Russians, including highly intelligent ones, don't believe and probably can't believe that freedom of the mind is that important. These Russians declare, and they are quite sincere, that their people are the freest in the world because they are not held down by caste, or class, or poverty. They will name men who are now high government officials, or managers of great industries, whose grandfathers were serfs. They will say that a Russian peasant boy has a far better chance of becoming head of one of the provincial governments than an American Negro has of becoming the governor of a State, and that is no lie. They will say that any boy who has brains, but no money, can secure an education free of charge in Russia, not only through the elementary schools, but through the universities and the professional schools as well. If he has the brains to make it, he may become a doctor, an engineer, a research scientist, or a scholar without paying a cent for tuition. They will wind up by saying that in Russia any career really is open to talent, regardless of money, and will ask how anyone could be freer, honestly believing that there is no answer.

An American may point out, however, that if a Russian stands up in public and declares that what the head of the state is doing is wrong and ruinous, as some Americans do every day about the President of the United States, that Russian would certainly be arrested, he probably would go to a Siberian forced-labor camp, and he would risk being hanged. But the Russian would probably say that freedom to call the President a fool is a pretty low kind of freedom and no intelligent man should set any value on it.

There are Americans—too many of them—who have no comeback to that line of argument. They are those Americans who, having been politically free all their lives, have seldom stopped to think seriously of what political freedom really means. Some think that it really does mean little more than the right to denounce any official they happen not to like. Others think that it means merely the right to make as much money as they can with the least possible effort. These Americans do not deserve freedom.

It isn't the right to denounce the President, or the right to do business in your own way that is valuable. It is the right to be heard and—for most of us far more important—the right to hear what others have to say, including those others whom the government may dislike intensely.

For we of the West have discovered one great truth that the Eastern nations have never come to believe. We did not do it through our superior wisdom and virtue. We discovered it the hard way, through centuries of suffering, through wars as useless as they were bloody, through making every mistake and committing every crime and folly that can be thought of. This is that great truth: *although any one man you may point out may be a foolish fellow, all the people, taken together, have a political wisdom that in the long run is superior to that of any one man.*

It follows that the state should always belong to the people, never the people to the state. The state is nothing more than the instrument they have chosen to, as our Declaration of Independence puts it, "effect their safety and happiness." If it fails to do that, the people have a right to cast it aside and set up another form of government. But they cannot make up their minds about the quality of their government without freely discussing it among themselves.

There is, after all, a comeback to the argument of the intelligent Russian who scorns our kind of freedom. It is comprised in one name. That name is Joseph Stalin, Lenin's successor.

Chapter 4

Stalin

Lenin was probably an ailing man when he came to Russia, and his tremendous efforts during the years of civil war were enough to break down a man who started in perfect health. At any rate, the first of the Communist dictators lived only seven years after he took control of the government. What happened in the Kremlin when Lenin died we don't know except for what Trotsky has told us, for it was carefully concealed from the rest of the world. Most of the West took it for granted that Trotsky would take Lenin's place and for a time it seemed that he had. But not for long. There was certainly a tremendous row, and certainly Trotsky lost the argument; for soon he was out and the man in charge was Joseph Stalin.

Lenin died in 1924, and during the next thirty years Stalin held all power in Russia; so for that long period his was the only brand of Communism that counted. It is reasonable, therefore, to say that if Marxism was the root of the system, and Leninism its flower, Stalinism was its fruit.

Joseph Stalin is not easy to describe. He had some of the qualities that go to make a great man, and many of those that go to make a villain. When he first came to power they were pretty evenly balanced, and it may be that the elements of greatness in his character weighed slightly more than the elements of villainy. In the Second World War his grim refusal to admit defeat was of tremendous value. But as time passed he grew worse and worse, instead of better and better, until at the end of his life there were strong reasons for believing that he was insane.

But nothing could be done about it. Stalin held power until he died. There is the answer to all arguments in favor of Communism.

Any system in which the people have only such power as the man at the top chooses to give them, instead of the man at the top having only such power as the people choose to give him, is likely at any time to produce such a ruler as Stalin. Great power, generally speaking, is not good for a man. Unless the people are free to remove a ruler who goes bad, every other kind of freedom is in danger. They are not free to do this under the Communist system; thus they hold all their other freedoms, not as rights, but as privileges that may be taken away if the dictator so decides.

Stalin was not Lenin's choice. Lenin never liked the man, but found him useful, especially when any dirty work had to be done. Trotsky quotes Lenin as having warned his associates several times to watch out for Stalin, because he was dangerous.

He was not a Russian. He came from Georgia, a province in the southeast corner of the czar's European realm. It is in part a wild, mountainous country, including the southern part of the Caucasus. Its southern boundary today is regarded as the line between Europe and Asia, and the Russians long looked upon the Georgians as more Asiatic than European. Stalin lived up to this reputation; as a ruler he undoubtedly resembled Genghis Khan more than Peter the Great. As a young man he had a wild career and seems to have been regarded as unusually tough, even for Georgia. Early in life he joined an anti-government faction that called itself the Communist party, although it seems to have been less a political party than a band of rowdies.

Exactly what Stalin did during those early days we do not know and never shall know, for in later years when he had become prominent and respectable he saw to it that all records, when there were any, were destroyed. His enemies say that he did worse, that he destroyed all witnesses, too. Thus we have little to go on but rumors, most of which cannot be regarded as reliable. However, one rumor that Stalin never cared to deny is that he kept the Georgian Communists supplied with funds by staging a series of bank robberies. Apparently he was rather proud of that, even though it gave his enemies an excuse for saying that most of the money stolen from the banks went into Stalin's pocket instead of into the party treasury. Judging by what he did later, there is little reason to assume that Joseph Stalin ever was a model young man, and it is possible he was a bandit.

How he managed to get himself elected Secretary of the Communist party nobody knows with certainty. Trotsky said that it was by the sneakiest kind of methods, including lies, bribery, and everything else detestable, but Trotsky was Stalin's mortal enemy at the time he wrote the history, which makes what he said rather doubtful.

Anyhow, Stalin was elected by the executive committee of the party, now known as the Presidium, which meant the men in the Kremlin—not the people of Russia, but the heads of the various departments of the government. How many members there were at that time is uncertain (there are now twenty-six), but it was a small group; yet with a majority of their votes Stalin won the secretaryship, which gave him supreme power. This seems rather odd to Americans. We should expect the president of the Supreme Soviet to be the chief man in Russia and the secretary a minor official, but it is another instance in which the Russians do things differently.

Later it became clear that Stalin's great desire was for power, and he hated poisonously any man who even threatened to become as powerful as he.

In addition to this personal feeling, there was one difference of opinion between him and Trotsky on an important matter of policy. The question was this: should the Communists try immediately to extend their system all over the world, or should they first try to strengthen it in Russia and extend it later? Trotsky said extend immediately, for such an opportunity might never come again. Stalin said no, build Communism in Russia first.

In 1917 Lenin certainly believed in worldwide revolution. The First World War had convinced him that the system of nationalism was cracking, and he thought it would collapse swiftly. It is in a moment of collapse and confusion that revolutionists have their chance as the Bolsheviks had theirs in 1917. But at the end of the war nationalism, while tottering, had not come down. So there is some reason to believe that before his death Lenin had begun to change his mind, and there is no doubt that some members of the executive committee had changed theirs. Nor is there much doubt that on this ground some members gave their votes to Stalin, although others may have been bribed or scared into doing so.

Be that as it may, when Stalin was made party secretary, Trotsky's policy of immediate, world-wide revolution was defeated. Others insisted that it was only postponed, for all sides agreed that Communism must sometime spread over the world; but the majority opposed pushing the extension until Russia had time to build up its own strength.

Yet although he was defeated in the committee, Trotsky was still a great man in the eyes of the people. If he had been hanged or shot immediately, the masses would have been so shocked that they might have lost all confidence in the government and, indeed, might have revolted against it. So Stalin proceeded against him cautiously, and it was in his dealing with Trotsky that his true character began to appear. It was not his doctrine, it was his popularity that made Trotsky hateful and dangerous to Stalin. Stalin believed absolutely what Machiavelli had said centuries before, that the only way for a man to retain power is by getting rid of every other man who is, or seems to be becoming, strong enough to take it away. Trotsky's strength lay in his popularity, hence it was necessary to destroy that before attacking the man himself.

Stalin began to undermine Trotsky one step at a time. First, he was removed from office. Second, the newspapers, magazines, radio, and all other means of publicity were forbidden to publish his writings. Third, Stalin's writers were set to denouncing all Trotsky's ideas as dangerous to the state, and these attacks were published by order everywhere. Then Trotsky was sent into exile. This was a mistake, for he was allowed to withdraw to the island of Prinkipo, now called Buyuk, in the Sea of Marmara, which was Turkish territory.

It was not long until Stalin realized that this was too close to Russia, so he demanded that Turkey expel the exile. Trotsky went to France, and when Stalin put the heat on France, to Mexico. Neither Turkey nor France wanted trouble with Russia, so, while they would not hand Trotsky over to the Russian police, they did advise him to move on. But Mexico didn't care, for there was no way by which Stalin could easily reach her. She allowed Trotsky to settle down and write as much as he pleased, and even gave him a police guard.

But Trotsky abroad proved more dangerous than he had been in Russia. He wrote not only his history of the Revolution, but a stream of newspaper and magazine articles denouncing Stalin as a betrayer of Leninism. Since the rest of the world had always regarded Trotsky as an authority on Communism second only to Lenin himself, Communist papers outside of Russia published these writings, and they produced enough of an effect to annoy Stalin greatly. He became determined to stop them. Since Mexico would not hand over Trotsky, and the Mexican police would not allow

any known Russian agent, or any man with a gun to get close to him, other means had to be devised. In 1940 a man disguised as a manual laborer slipped into the house and murdered Trotsky by beating him on the head with a pickax.

That was a sample of the way Stalin governed Russia for nearly thirty years. He moved carefully at first, with some regard for public opinion. The murder of Trotsky was a brutal and disgusting crime, but Stalin denied responsibility for it. It was a fact, however, that Trotsky was dangerous to Stalin's power, and he was killed to remove that danger. Many years later it began to appear that Trotsky may have been more dangerous to Stalinism than even Stalin guessed. Nearly twenty-five years after the murder the world discovered that one of the men Trotsky seems to have convinced was Mao Tse-tung, the Chinese Communist leader, and his followers have continued to proclaim Trotskyism to the embarrassment of Stalin's successor.

The world might abhor, although it could understand, the murder of Trotsky, but as the years passed Stalin's crimes continued with less and less cause that any normal person could see. More and more men began to disappear. Among the first to go were those who were known as the Old Bolsheviks, that is, the men who had worked with Lenin during and even before the Revolution of 1917. These men had become national heroes, regarded in Russia somewhat as Americans regard the men who helped and worked with George Washington in 1776.

The Old Bolsheviks' crime was that they had been close to Lenin, and it was natural for ordinary Russians to suppose that they knew what he thought and what he intended better than anyone else, better than Stalin who, in Lenin's time, had been away down toward the bottom of the list of prominent leaders.

These national heroes had to go, and one by one, but later in groups, they went. An especially horrible part of this purge was that it was not enough simply to kill them; they had to be made detestable in the eyes of the people before they were killed. This was done by putting them to torture, not the old-fashioned kind — beating, burning with red-hot irons, and the like — but a smoother kind that left no traces. If a man is beaten or branded there will be marks and scars showing that he has been tortured, and everyone will know that his confession doesn't mean anything. Stalin's torturers worked out more subtle and less visible means — denying water to the prisoner, denying him food, never letting him sleep, shutting him in a cage too small to allow him to sit or stand or lie comfortably, and always asking questions, always talking, always threatening, until he was driven out of his right mind, yet without showing any bruises or scars.

Then they would bring the prisoner to trial, and he would say anything they wanted him to say. He would confess to having sold military secrets to foreign nations, to having robbed the state, to having plotted to overthrow the government, to anything. If the torture had been skillfully applied for a long enough time, the man's mind might be broken to the point at which he actually believed, at least for the time, that he had done those things. In any case, when he publicly confessed to the most dreadful crimes, his execution seemed to be just.

This technique was effective in three ways. First, it enabled Stalin to get rid of any man who might be thinking of trying to pull him down. Second, it terrified any others who might be thinking of trying to pull him down. Third, and most important of all, it gave the common people the impression that the country swarmed with spies and traitors, even on the highest levels, and they could trust nobody but Stalin to save Russia from being sold to her enemies. It was a type of villainy new to the modern world. Murder was an old familiar story. Despots had always been given to murder. Nor was blackening the victim's character anything new. Murderous rulers always tried to make it appear that their victims were guilty of terrible crimes. But the process of making a man destroy his own reputation—killing his own good name before his body was killed—was something far worse than murder.

Disgracing and murdering his enemies, however, did not remove all of Stalin's difficulties. Still the government was faced with that terrible problem of feeding the people. Lenin's New Economic Policy had done much toward persuading the peasants to produce more, but at that they were not producing enough, and the factory workers in the cities were so poorly fed that in some places they staged dangerous riots. As for the peasants, they were still dissatisfied. The government claimed a large quota of all the food they produced, and they could sell nothing until they had delivered that quota. After they set aside what they needed to feed themselves and their households, they were often left with nothing to sell.

As a result, large numbers of peasants decided to raise just enough food for their own use and stop with that. Unfortunately for them, they were not dealing with the relatively civilized Lenin, who knew much about the outside world, but with a barbarous Georgian who had never left Russia and never cared to go. He didn't even know much of Russia — he seldom talked to factory workers and never visited the country villages, as Lenin often did, to see with his own eyes what the peasants' life was like. He stayed in the Kremlin and issued orders. When harvest time came he sent his collectors to the farms with soldiers behind them and seized the government quota. If

that left the peasant with nothing, or not enough to feed his family during the winter, it was just too bad for him. The food was removed to the cities and the peasant left to starve. It is estimated that not less than two million died of famine during these years.

As Stalin grew older his rule became more and more bloody, with less and less reason, as outsiders saw it. It is characteristic of a man whose nature is suspicious to begin with to grow more and more suspicious as he grows older, and in Stalin's case it went beyond the bounds of sanity. There is

much reason to believe that in his last years he was nothing short of a madman.

Little more than a year before the outbreak of the Second World War he conceived the idea that the military high command had begun to plot against him. In view of his character it is easily possible that it may have been true, but the evidence, if there was any, has never been made public, so the rest of the world doesn't know. All it knows is that very suddenly there were a great many missing generals who have not been seen since and therefore are presumed to be dead. Military experts are divided about the effects of this procedure; some think that Stalin killed off his best commanders, which explains why the Russian army made such a poor showing in the first part of the fighting. If so, he nearly lost the war before it started. A more cynical view is that by killing the incompetents he made room at the top for the men who finally stopped the German advance.

However, the most terrible injury inflicted upon Russia by Stalin's strange mentality came in 1939 when, for reasons unknown to the rest of the world, he decided that Great Britain and France, presumably with the connivance of the United States, were conspiring to destroy Russia. This suspicion betrayed him into an act nothing short of madness. He trusted the one man nobody else in the world dreamed of trusting — Adolf Hitler.

In 1939 he signed with Hitler a document which was called a nonaggression pact, but which was in essence an agreement to split Poland between Nazi Germany and Communist Russia, each of the robbers swearing not to deprive the other of his part of the loot. Of course, as soon as Hitler had defeated France, and mistakenly thought he had defeated Britain, he fell upon Russia. He swept through all of Poland and far into Russia. He was not stopped until he had reached the Volga River and had brought infinite misery to the Russian people.

The question repeats itself as one goes down the long list of crimes and follies committed by the Stalin government — why did the people endure him for so many years without a revolt, without any serious opposition?

Part of the answer is easy: they did not know

what was going on. But when you proceed to ask why they did not know, the answer is far from simple. It goes beyond the set-up of the Soviet government. It touches the conviction, drilled into Russians by centuries of despotism, that the people belong to the state, not the state to the people; hence the state must control the people, minds and bodies, because for the people to control the state would be ruinous.

The way in which it was managed is simple enough. The people did not know what was going on because the government did not want them to know, and controlled every means by which they might have found out. Printing, mails, radio, telegraph and telephone lines were all in the hands of the government and were allowed to transmit only such news as the government chose to give out. On the other hand, all these agencies were compelled to transmit what the government did give out. For example, when Stalin made a speech every newspaper in Russia had to print it, every radio station had to repeat it, and millions of copies were sent through the mails. But if the President of the United States made a speech denying what Stalin said, not a word of it was heard in Russia.

When two million peasants starved to death because the government men had carried away the food, nothing was said about it in the newspapers or on radio or elsewhere. Of course, rumors got around, but they were vague and uncertain. Most people knew that there was some kind of trouble with the peasants. They might even have known that in a certain village from which someone had recently come there had been one or two or half-a-dozen deaths from starvation; and they might have guessed that something of the kind was happening in other places, but they did not actually know. To this day many Russians have not heard that the deaths reached the appalling number of two million, and when they are told they do not believe it.

After the Second World War the United States, whose territory had not been trampled by the battling armies, offered to help the war-damaged nations rebuild their smashed factories and railroads and highways and bridges, so that they could more quickly get back to peaceful living. This scheme was called the Marshall Plan, after the Secretary of State who announced it. The offer was made to Russia, just as to the other nations that had been damaged. But Stalin's government not only refused the offer, it told the Russian people that it was not a real offer to help, it was a plot by American millionaires who hoped to gain control of everything valuable in Russia. The reason for telling such a lie was fear that, in dealing with American agents of the Marshall Plan, the Russians might learn that capitalism is not as bad as they had supposed; therefore, there must be no such dealing.

Winston Churchill gave us the phrase for it. He said that an Iron Curtain had come down between Russia and the rest of the world, and the policy has been known as the Iron Curtain ever since.

France and Great Britain, our friends in the late war, did accept the Marshall Plan. Germany, recently our enemy, did too, and all three rebuilt their damaged industries very rapidly without turning them over to American millionaires. Russia was offered aid on exactly the same terms, and to us it seems that she might have done equally well. Why, then, didn't she take it?

Now we come down to the thing that makes Communism, or at least Russian Communism, an impossible form of government for a nation of freemen. Russia couldn't accept Marshall Plan aid without giving up her whole theory of government. That theory holds that the capitalist system is by its very nature vicious and can't be anything else, and because it is so thoroughly vicious it is bound to destroy itself at last and that is how Communism will conquer the whole world. To accept the Marshall Plan would have been to admit that the capitalistic system can sometimes do the wise and decent thing; and if sometimes, why not many times? To the men in the Kremlin it was more important to keep the Russians persuaded that Communism was their only hope than it was to restore peace and prosperity quickly. In short, the state, not a thing but a political idea, must be preserved no matter at what cost to the people.

From the standpoint of men whose chief aim is to keep power in their own hands — and Stalin was such a man — they were right. But from the standpoint of men whose chief aim is to make this a better world — and Marx was such a man — they were entirely wrong. Keeping the people in ignorance of what is happening in the world beyond the horizon is not Marxism. All his life Marx insisted that the only way the common people could gain real freedom was by constantly reading, studying, debating, and thinking. The opposite idea is not Marxian; it is entirely Russian.

Yet it is not hard to see why the Russians felt that the people should be told only what some authority thought was good for them to know. They had never known any other system. For hundreds of years they had been ruled by men whose aim was to keep power in their own hands, and secrecy is a great help in holding on to power.

Lenin had approved of Western ideas as far as Western science was concerned. But Lenin was convinced that Western political ideas were thoroughly bad, and he had no intention of allowing them to be introduced into Russia. Marx was responsible for this, for he believed it, too; and this leads us to the great error of Karl Marx, the one point on which he has been proved wrong not by the arguments of his opponents, but by the history of the past century.

Chapter 5

Today and Tomorrow

Marx, seeing that working conditions in his time were bad in capitalist countries, and having no hope that greed could ever be removed from the hearts of men, drew a logical if harsh conclusion. He prophesied that in time conditions would get so bad that there would be a revolt of the workers that would destroy the capitalist system.

Marx was definitely against the use of violence as a means of advancing the fall of capitalism. Its own inner faults, he said, would eventually kill it; therefore, the policy of Communists should be to let those faults develop rapidly, not to try to establish Communism by force before capitalism was already as good as dead.

His error was in failing to take into account the possibility that capitalism itself was passing through a phase that would not last forever, and that the evils he saw were a part of the passing phase, not of capitalism. If that were true, they could and probably would be corrected in the next phase, without the necessity of destroying the whole system. He is hardly to be blamed for ignoring this possibility, since it is only in recent years that economists in general have begun to consider it; but an error it was, as the last hundred years have proved.

The hard, solid fact is that the plight of the workers in advanced capitalist countries did not continue to grow worse. On the contrary, it began to get better before Marx died, and it has continued to improve except when it has suffered a temporary setback due to some definite cause, such as war, or the great depression of the nineteen thirties. Communism, instead of taking over the advanced countries of western Europe and America, first took over the most backward, industrially, of them all — Russia — and has since spread only into China, even more backward than Russia.

Many explanations of the improvement of workers' conditions in capitalist countries have been offered. Some of them are pure nonsense, but others do explain part, although not the whole, of this development. Much was done by men and women in the capitalist countries to remedy the worst evils. They acted, not on any economic theory, but because they were sickened by such indecencies as having women in harness dragging loaded cars in coal mines through shafts so low that they had to crawl on hands and knees; and putting children to work in textile factories at ten, and eight, and even six years old. Much was done by organizing the workers into unions powerful enough to bargain with employers on equal terms. Much was done by wise statesmen, who enacted laws forbidding brutal treatment of workers and holding employers responsible for deaths and injuries suffered in their industrial plants.

But make careful note of this: the men and women who exposed and protested against the scandals, the organizers who built up the labor unions, and the statesmen who enacted the reform laws, all achieved their partial success by creating a strong public opinion that demanded action; and they were able to create that opinion because they could tell the people, by writing books and newspaper articles, by making speeches, by talking face to face, just what was going on and how villainous it was. Without the right of free speech they could have done little, if anything.

But with that right they were able gradually to persuade employers, on the one hand, that indecent working conditions were not only wrong, but foolish; and, on the other hand, to persuade workers that by combining they could improve their condition without upsetting the whole economic and political system. Thus, little by little, the American economic system has taken over many of the really good ideas in Marx's great book, *Capital,* while rejecting the chief error of the book — the error of believing that capitalism could not improve, but must be torn down completely.

The process, of course, is still going on and will continue for many years, since nothing in this world is ever made perfect. Radicals constantly cry out that it is far too slow, that we are still wedded to the ideas of feudalism; conservatives cry just as loudly that it is far too fast, that we are on the verge of socialism. But most of us have felt, thus far, that we are doing fairly well and should neither try to halt social change, nor try to drive it too fast.

When Joseph Stalin died in 1953, a sigh of relief went up from the other members of the Presidium, but nobody outside the Kremlin knew it, for the insiders agreed they must put up a false front. Later we learned that they had been living in terror of their lives, but in 1953 they felt that if they made public their real opinion of the dictator, the Russian people would be so shocked that they might bring down the whole Soviet structure. So they concealed their joy and put on a spectacle of public mourning such as the world has seldom seen.

They embalmed Stalin's body and put it in the same tomb with that of Lenin. This was more than a funeral. It resembled the ceremony in ancient Rome by which a dead Caesar was elevated to a place among the gods, for Lenin's tomb is unlike any other place in all Russia. It is not a grave, it is a mausoleum, a flat-topped structure of black marble in Moscow's Red Square; in it the body lies in a coffin with a glass lid so that it may be seen by

visitors — it is not far from the truth to call them worshipers — who come by the thousands every year.

On the flat top of the tomb the highest officers of the state take their stand on solemn occasions, to review parades and to address the people on May Day, the chief Communist holiday, or whenever an announcement of great importance is to be made. It is the most venerated shrine in Russia, and putting Stalin's body there was the highest honor the Russians could pay to any man.

But it was all a fake. Three years later, at the Twentieth Congress of the Soviet Communist Party, Nikita S. Khrushchev, who had taken Stalin's place as secretary of the party, spoke for seven hours and devoted a large part of the time to telling the truth about Stalin. It was a secret session, held in February, 1956, and not until June was the full text of the speech published in this country, but the main points became known in Russia soon after the Congress adjourned.

It was a terrific attack. To be sure, Khrushchev said not a word about some of the worst things Stalin did, such as the murder of Trotsky, and he touched lightly on the deliberate starvation of two million peasants. But he tore into Stalin for having twisted the doctrine of Marx and Lenin into an excuse for becoming a tyrant worse than most czars. Khrushchev carefully left out the fact that the Soviet doctrine of thought control is what makes such tyranny possible.

Naturally the speech was a sensation. It startled the rest of the world almost as much as it did the Russians, and for a time many people in the democracies believed that the whole Communist system was about to blow up, especially when, shortly after Khrushchev's speech, they removed Stalin's body from the mausoleum and buried it in an ordinary grave alongside some minor Communist leaders. But the system didn't collapse. Khrushchev managed to take over a large part of Stalin's power and for at least ten years ruled Russia successfully.

One reason for his success abroad, and perhaps at home too, was that he baffled all efforts to understand him. It was plain from the start that he was different from the other dictators, but the Western nations have never been able to make up their minds as to just what the difference signifies. Lenin and Stalin were both solemn fellows. Khrushchev laughed and joked. Lenin looked as sour as a very strict schoolmaster, Stalin as grim as the chief gunman for some American gangster mob; but Khrushchev, bald and rather below medium height, was roly-poly, reminding one of a slightly comic Buddha. Lenin and Stalin stayed apart from people, rarely admitting visitors, especially foreigners. Khrushchev startled outsiders by running about everywhere and talking to anybody; in two visits to the United States he talked to the President and the Secretary of State, of course, but also to farmers, factory workers, businessmen, school children, and anybody else he happened to meet.

Sometimes he was jolly and good-humored, sometimes outrageous. He met Vice-President Nixon at a fair in Moscow, and they yelled at each other like a pair of taxi drivers after a collision. He sat with the Russian delegation at the United Nations once, and when someone made a speech that he didn't like, he not only shouted his disapproval, but pulled off a shoe and beat on the desk with it.

by the Poles in June, and by the Hungarians in October. Both were crushed by Russian tanks and soldiers. Stalin could not have done it more ruthlessly.

Nevertheless, the world could soon see differences between Stalin and Khrushchev. The old love of secrecy still remained, and no doubt will as long as the rulers continue to believe that they must govern the thoughts as well as the acts of the people. On account of that secrecy we can never know exactly what the situation is in the Kremlin, but there are reasons to believe that Khrushchev is by no means as absolute as Stalin was. More than once he has started along a certain line, then suddenly abandoned it, although nobody outside Russia forced him to do so, and he must have been compelled from inside. It is reasonable to assume that the other men in the Kremlin put the pressure on him, because nobody else could have done it.

This soon led outside observers, or some of them, to guess that one-man rule is out. They think that the system has now become what the experts call "collegial," that is, rule by a group of colleagues, rather than by one man. This may be —

which is not to say that it must be — an improvement. In times past rule by a group — an oligarchy — has sometimes, but not always, been better than rule by a single despot. It is generally agreed that ten years after the death of Stalin the average Russian was somewhat better off than he had been before.

To say, though, that there has been any important change in the Communist system is to go far beyond the known facts. It has changed, of course. Everything in the world has changed somewhat since 1917. By wind and weather Mount Washington and Pike's Peak have suffered some erosion in fifty years, but they are still there. So is Communism—perhaps chipped off a bit here and there, but still a huge and heavy fact that cannot be ignored by the nations that believe in freedom.

It is certain, however, that Khrushchev knows more about the outside world than Stalin did. He has traveled much, and has talked face-to-face, not only with the free world's leading statesmen, but with writers, artists, businessmen, and wage-earners beyond the boundaries of Russia. If he makes a fatal mistake, it will be because he misjudged the facts, not because he never heard of them.

It is fairly certain, too, that Trotsky's idea that Communism could and should conquer the world by military force is not held by Khrushchev. The hydrogen bomb has made military conquest too expensive. In a nuclear war both sides would take such a terrible beating that "victory" would not be worth a fraction of what it cost.

But Khrushchev is an ingenious fellow, far more so than Stalin. He has found ways of extending Communist influence without war. Wherever the masses of the people are living in poverty and misery, he can go in, as he did in Cuba, offering all kinds of beautiful promises and sometimes giving real help. So he persuades the people themselves to turn to Communism without conquest from outside. This is a kind of strategy that the democratic nations find hard to meet. Their only chance is to beat the Communists to it, and that is expensive, so short-sighted people are slow to try it. The United States has given more aid than any other democracy, but at that we didn't get to Cuba in time. We tolerated the dreadful Batista regime so long that it had made the Cubans desperate and ready to follow Castro into the Communist camp.

There is another reason why Khrushchev has to watch his step more carefully than Stalin did. It is the rise of Communist China, a nation that has enormous manpower, and is believed to have set off an atomic explosion in 1963. A nation that has learned to produce an atomic explosion can learn to make an atomic bomb.

The trouble with China, as the Russians see it, is that Chinese Communism is more Trotskyite than Leninist. That is to say, the Chinese seem to believe, as Trotsky did, that Communism ought to be pushed forward all over the world, by war if necessary. In the beginning Lenin thought so, too, but before his death he realized that it couldn't be done that way, which has been the prevailing opinion in Russia since. But if the Chinese start on world conquest, the Russians may be dragged into a fight for which they are not prepared.

Furthermore, the Russians have had drilled into them for centuries — long before Communism was heard of — the belief that it is extremely dangerous to trust any other nation. In Asia the boundary line between Russia and China is about 3000 miles long, far too long to be defended at every point. If Russia became involved in a great war in the West, could the Chinese be trusted not to cross that boundary and seize Siberia while Russia was too busy to do anything about it? Khrushchev certainly does not want to take that risk, if he can avoid it.

These facts explain why, although he loses no chance to abuse the United States in the most violent terms, Khrushchev let ten years pass without making war upon us. But that is no great comfort if he can weaken us without making war. He failed in the Congo, and for five years had little success with the Arabs in the Middle East; but he did much better in Cuba, and by 1963 was plainly making progress in the rest of Latin America.

While it seems probable that the Russian people are better off under Khrushchev than they were under Stalin, it is far from certain that the milder dictator is less dangerous to the rest of the world than the fiercer one was. Khrushchev may not be able to destroy our liberty by force, but if he can make the rest of the world think liberty is a sham, and cause even some Americans to lose faith in it, he will have accomplished his purpose without firing a shot.

When Stalin refused our offer of help under the Marshall Plan, some Americans decided that the man must be crazy, but they failed to take into account his situation. Stalin was a dictator, and he proposed to remain a dictator. Perhaps the very fact that a man wishes to be a dictator is proof that he is crazy. But if he is one, and proposes to remain in power, it is not insanity but good sense for him to keep his people as far as possible from any friendly contact with a nation of freemen.

For almost all men have two deep and strong desires. They wish to be safe, and they wish to manage their own affairs as they see fit. Security and liberty are two desires that seem to be common to every kind of man — white, black, red, yellow, or brown.

Now a dictator, or any other despot, finds it easiest to rule people who are terrified by some danger that they regard as more dreadful than the despot. The danger may be real, or it may be only fancied, but as long as the people believe it to be real, and that the despot is their one protection against it, they will endure his rule, forgetting or suppressing their desire to be free.

Stalin was highly successful in persuading the Russians to believe that all the rest of the world, especially the United States, was plotting their destruction. If the truth must be told, we gave him some help. For forty years we have been rough on Communists, because we are just as sure of their determination to destroy us as they are of our determination to destroy them.

The writer of this book has never yet encountered an American who believes that it is our purpose or our wish to destroy the Russians, but many Americans feel sure that the time will come when we shall have to fight them. If we fight with nuclear weapons, we cannot avoid killing many millions, including great numbers of women and children, sick persons, and men too old to serve in the army. We shall have to do it to be certain of killing enough soldiers to win the war. It is a sickening idea, but what else can we do if they are determined to destroy us?

That is the state of affairs called the cold war. From our side, the whole thing is a fraud, because the Russians fear something that doesn't exist, namely an American desire and purpose to wipe them out. But while the danger may be imaginary, the fear is real, and all the world knows that a terrified man is a dangerous man with a gun, because he is likely to start shooting when there is no need to shoot. As long as the Russians remain terrified, we must remain on guard, which in the modern world means spending fifty billion dollars or more on armament every year.

Who benefits by the cold war? Chiefly, the Soviet government. The word "chiefly" is inserted because some people in this country benefit somewhat. For instance, except for the cold war our armed forces would not have to be so large, and a number of generals would have to find other jobs. Some politicians, too, might fail to be elected if they were not able, by howling against Communists, to divert attention from their own failures. But by far the largest number involved are the many thousands who are employed in making weapons and other military supplies. If these people all lost their jobs at once, the results would be serious.

All this, however, we could endure, for there would be no great danger of its upsetting the government. But in Russia an end of the cold war would almost certainly result in changes that would amount to a collapse of the whole system, and the men in the Kremlin would be crushed under the ruins.

The reason is simple. If they no longer feared America, the Russians would feel reasonably safe, certainly much safer than they feel now. But as their desire for security was satisfied, that other desire of all mankind would rise to the top — they would begin to long for liberty. Hence it is to the interest of the Communist government to keep them frightened, and events have played into their hands. The United States does have enormous military power, and the Russians for centuries have learned the hard way that power inevitably means tyranny. If they ever discovered that it is possible for the people of a nation to control their own government and still be strong and prosperous, that is, to enjoy both security and liberty, they would inevitably demand both, and the present system of Communism could not last long. Hence they must not be allowed to make the discovery.

Looked at from one angle it would seem that two great nations are being pushed into a war that would heavily damage, if not destroy, both, not because there is any real necessity to fight, but because a false necessity has been created. That would be the greatest absurdity in all history if it were true, but it is not exactly true. There is a real necessity for taking this risk, the necessity of the men in control of the Russian government. Without the pressure exerted by deadly fear their control could not be maintained; hence the fear must be kept alive and the United States is the logical object of that fear.

History has made it so. Lenin was quite right in assuming that the old system of nationalism was cracking up, but that was a system of national imperialism. Before 1914 there were seven nations commonly accepted as the great powers. They were Britain, Germany, Russia, Austro-Hungary, France, Japan, and the United States. Each was an empire in the sense that it held control of territory not within its strictly national boundaries. Even the United States held the Philippines. Since 1945 there have been just two that rate as really great powers. They are Russia and the United States. The empires have not only cracked, they have crashed. So far, Lenin was right.

But that was national imperialism. As for nationalism in the strict sense, far from collapsing, it has spread like a brush fire all over the world. The United Nations today has more than fifty brand-new members. Yet think of the situation that these new nations face. The collapse of imperialism has not destroyed power, it has only caused it to collect around two opposing centers, Washington and Moscow. The new nations are composed of people who have been accustomed for centuries to tie together power and tyranny. Their experience has taught them that a powerful nation is invariably a tyrannous nation. Hence what they see in Washington and Moscow is a double concentration of tyranny, not, perhaps, as of this moment but certain to be just that in the future. This accounts for the neutralism of nations that, like India, have recently gained independence. It enrages Americans that such nations admit no moral distinction between our democracy and Russian Communism, but the indignation is misplaced. If our moral superiority is invisible to everyone except us, indignation is of no help.

It may be perfectly true that the American people have no intention and no ambition either to destroy the Russians or to rule over any of the new nations, but that isn't the point. The point is that those nations believe something quite different. They believe that any nation having power will certainly use it in the way that power has always been used, unless the strong nation is restrained by some equal and opposite power.

History is with them. Concentrated power has, in fact, been used exactly as they say it has. It is logic then, not malice, that makes them feel that if Washington is their protection against Moscow, then Moscow is no less their protection against Washington. Neutralism, the desire not to be tied up with either side, is perfectly natural to small, weak nations.

It is the belief of the Western nations, and of America in particular, that democracy is a more intelligent form of government than any other that has been tried when, but only when, it is based on freedom of the mind, which can't exist without freedom of speech, of the press, and of worship. Where freedom of the mind exists, we believe that imperialism cannot endure permanently. There may be exceptions; there are areas in which the people have so little knowledge of the art of government that they cannot make democracy work; but it is our belief that these areas are already small and rapidly shrinking.

It follows that while we do have enormous military and economic power, wise Americans are opposed to using it imperially. Under the old faith that power must always be used to extend dominion, there would be nothing for it but for us to fight the Russians, since theirs is the only power that comes close to equaling ours. But there are two reasons against it. The Industrial Revolution has taken the profit out of dominion. That is the first reason. The second is that war has become ruinously expensive. An intelligent man does not desire property that costs more to keep up than it can possibly bring in, and to ruin himself in the effort to acquire such property would not be the act of an intelligent man, but of a lunatic.

Thus we have developed a new faith — that the only intelligent use of military power is for defense against attack. That faith is based on what happened in 1945. On August 6 in that year the whole nature of international war was changed. Up to that time victory in war was won at the moment when the enemy's will to fight was destroyed. But when the first atom bomb exploded over Hiroshima, the object of war became to destroy the enemy, not merely his will to fight. With such a weapon it is impossible to take aim at the enemy's army; everything within its range will be destroyed—women, children, babies in their cradles, and cripples in their wheelchairs, as well as soldiers under arms. The object of such a weapon is not to break the enemy's will to fight, but to exterminate his whole population — not victory, but massacre.

Of course, what you do to the enemy, he will do to you, if he can; and if he is a powerful enemy, he can do so much that the end of a nuclear war would probably be the destruction of both the combatants. Since 1945 we have developed bombs so powerful that they make the one dropped on Hiroshima seem little more than a toy. Of the 353,000 people in Hiroshima that day, three fourths survived; but if it had been a 1964-model hydrogen bomb it is unlikely that a single human being in Hiroshima would have been left alive.

Russia has such bombs. Britain has them. France is making them. China has produced atomic explosions, the first long step toward the bomb. For the United States willfully to start a war in which they would be used would be an act of sheer madness. We know it, but does anybody else know that we know it? The Russians certainly don't, or the Chinese; and there is doubt that many of the neutral nations are convinced that we can be relied on to act like sane people.

That is the situation that the United States faces, and anyone who thinks it is not serious has lost his wits.

But if not war, then what? Are we simply to sit still, allowing Communism to spread through the earth with no opposition of any kind?

Of course, what we must do is not entirely within our power to decide. In part it depends on what the Communists do, and what that will be we can do no more than guess. But an informed guess is usually better than a guess in the dark, and perhaps the best-informed guessers are the Harvard people who have made a careful study of the Soviet system. They see four possible roads, any one of which the Russians may take within the next five or ten years.

The first is the road back to Stalinism. This seems the least likely, because the Russians have had one heavy dose of Stalinism and it has made them pretty sick. Yet under Communism that kind of thing is always possible.

The second leads to a gradual increase in the power of the men who manage the great industries. As a class, they are interested first in producing the goods, and only second in spreading the doctrines of Marxism-Leninism.

The third goes toward an increase not of nationalism, but of racism, the old czarist notion that the Slavs are destined to be the master race, Communist or not. That would mean trouble on a large scale, because it is not rational, and might be crazy enough to start a nuclear war.

The fourth is toward a gradual change, a sort of evolution, of the Soviet system that would bring it nearer and nearer to the political ideals of the Western world. This is the one we should hope for, but we must face the fact that progress in that direction will be so slow as to strain our patience to the breaking point.

What we shall have to do depends in part on which of these four directions Russia takes. But we should be foolish indeed to allow our course to be determined entirely by what the Communists do. It is plain that our policy should be designed to push the Russians in the direction of the fourth road, but exactly how we are to do that is not easy to say. It is, in truth, so hard a problem that it gives sleepless nights to our wisest statesmen and political experts.

Russia is there, and going to be there as far as we can see into the future; and as long as she is we shall have to deal with her, which requires action. But action is not required of you and me. We have a man to whom the job is delegated. If he makes a botch of it, at a stated time we can remove him and choose another; but as long as he is there it is not only unwise, it is unlawful, to interfere with what he does.

That man is the President of the United States, to whom the Constitution delegates the sole right to conduct the foreign affairs of this nation. Even the Senate, although it can stop the President from making what it considers an unwise treaty, cannot compel him to do anything, nor can the Supreme Court.

This book, however, is not written for the President of the United States and his advisers, but for plain ordinary Americans who hold no political office and aspire to none. Especially it is written for young Americans, who have little to say in public affairs today, but who will have great voting power a few years hence. What should we ordinary private citizens do right now about Communism?

A freeman must understand the essential importance of his right to think, to hear what others are thinking, and to make up his own mind as to what is true. Yet there are many, far too many,

Americans who cannot bring themselves to believe that this right is so important that it must be defended at all costs. In that, they are lining up with the Communists at the very point where the Communists are most certainly and most dangerously wrong. These fearful Americans fall into that error, because they do not know what Communism really is, and they will never get out of the error until they set themselves to learn the facts.

Yet most of them will not learn and — this is what makes them dangerous — they make every effort to prevent others from learning. They object

as violently to any careful study of capitalism. Yet in many parts of this country if a public school teacher begins to tell a class how Communism works, certain people will accuse him of trying to make Communists of his pupils, when he is doing exactly the opposite.

These people cannot seem to realize that the poison in Communism is its suppression of the search for truth, the whole truth, not only that part that suits our purposes. The whole truth about Communism includes the fact that it has worked in Russia for nearly fifty years, that it has taken over China, that it has spread through Cuba, and that it is attractive to many people in Asia, Africa, and South America. These facts do not prove that it is a good system; but they must be taken into account before one can explain why, in spite of these facts, it is bad.

Until we understand what is good about Communism, and why the evil in it outweighs the good, we shall never contrive an effective defense against it. For Communism isn't a thing, it is an idea. This is what short-sighted Americans can't get through their heads. What they really believe is that Communism is the Red Army, and therefore is to be fought in the same way that you would fight any other army. But if you try to fight an idea in the same way that you would fight an army, you will certainly lose, for you can't blast an idea with a multi-megaton bomb, or shoot it down with the most ingenious anti-missile missile.

This is not to deny that the Red Army is a danger, but the job of handling the Red Army, if it ever becomes necessary, will not be in the hands of ordinary citizens, who have no responsibility for the details of our defense plans.

We are responsible for the defeat, not of the Red Army, but of the Communist idea. Freedom of person can and must be defended by the armed forces; a soldier with a gun is a danger, but that danger can be met and mastered by a better soldier with a better gun. A false idea, however, is a greater danger, and the best soldier with the best gun can do nothing about it; it can be met and mastered only by a better, which is to say a true, idea.

In this imperfect world it is highly doubtful that anybody knows all the truth about anything; but men have learned by bitter experience that, while we may never reach absolute truth about a problem as complicated as government, the one way to come closer to it is to study all the relevant and available facts. That is impossible without freedom of the mind.

The will *not* to know is calamity, for it is cowardice, and a coward cannot be a freeman, nor can a nation overcome by its fears ever be free. If we should come to the point at which we decide that freedom of speech must be denied, we shall then and there be enslaved by our fears.

This is the present condition of the Russian people, and because of that condition they are a danger to themselves and to all the rest of the world. For when they prohibit the free activity of the mind, they turn themselves into a roadblock across the only path by which mankind has made any real and valuable progress.

No man ever gave freedom to another man. Still less did any nation ever make another nation free. The most that one can do for a slave is to strike off his chains; then he is emancipated, but he is not yet a freeman and he never will be one except by his own will and deed. Russia cannot be made free by military conquest. Freedom must be sought; it cannot be imposed.

For emphasis, be it repeated that what follows is not for the President, or for anyone charged with special duties in the realm of public affairs, but for the plain American who holds no political office and seeks none. This man also has a duty. Those others are charged with defense of the nation, but it is the plain American who is charged with the defense of liberty, and he can defend it only by being free.

It follows that when an American, for fear or favor, stands silent when he ought to speak what he believes to be truth; when, for fear or favor, he gives consent to denial of another American's rights; when, for fear or favor, he assents to forcible suppression of ideas he does not approve; when, for fear or favor, he shuts his ears to men he knows to be honest if they try to tell him disagreeable truths — that American is deserting his post and leaving a gap through which Communism may creep into this country.

By the same token, when an American defends

and boldly exercises his freedom to think, to learn, and to proclaim the truth, he demonstrates the ability of freemen to attain liberty and security at the same time. Every such demonstration is a deadly blow at Communism.

Important Dates in the History of Communism

1818—Karl Marx born (died 1883).
1847—Marx and Engels issue *Communist Manifesto.*
1849—Marx expelled from Germany.
1867—First volume of *Capital* (others, 1885, 1895).
1870—Lenin born.
1879—Stalin born.
1914—Russia enters First World War.
1917—Bolsheviks seize power in Russia (November).
1918—Treaty of Brest-Litovsk (March 3).
1921—Russian civil war ends.
1921—Lenin's New Economic Policy.
1922—Stalin becomes secretary-general of Communist party.
1924—Lenin dies.
1929—Trotsky banished, Stalin's power consolidated.
1936—Purges of Communist party.
1937—Purges of army.
1939—Stalin's pact with Hitler.
1940—Trotsky murdered.
1941—Hitler invades Russia.
1953—Stalin dies, Khrushchev becomes first secretary of Communist party.
1956—Stalin degraded.
1956—Polish and Hungarian revolts.
1958—Khrushchev becomes premier.
1963—Conference at Moscow reveals serious differences between Russia and China.

GERALD W. JOHNSON was born in Riverton, North Carolina, and received his B.A. from Wake Forest College in North Carolina. He is married and has two daughters, also married. At present he and his wife are living in Baltimore, where he works as a free-lance newspaper man when he is not writing a book.

Mr. Johnson has had a long and distinguished career in journalism. Since 1911, he has worked on a number of Southern newspapers, including the *Baltimore Evening Sun* (1926-1939), and he was a news commentator on WAAM-TV. He was also Professor of Journalism at the University of North Carolina and a contributing editor for *The New Republic*. He is the author of over twenty books, including the well-known *Andrew Jackson, Incredible Tale*, and *The Lunatic Fringe*. Almost every book he has written deals with some aspect of his favorite subject, American history. The trilogy, *America, a History for Peter*, is his first work on the subject for young people. It was followed by a second trilogy entitled *The Government*, which included *The Presidency, The Supreme Court*, and *The Congress*.

Knowledge of our history, Mr. Johnson believes, inevitably leads to an increased understanding of the rest of the world; and to understand other nations is the heaviest responsibility weighing upon the rising generation of Americans.

Index

*Indicates illustrations

R

Red Army, 72, 89, 151
Red Russians, 43, 70*-71*
Reformation, 51-52, 56
Renaissance, 50, 52, 56
Roman Empire, 49-50, 52
Rumania, 78
Russian Revolution, 14, 22, 32, 37, 38*-39*, 65, 73, 99*

S

Sansculottes, 67-68, 82
Savonarola, Girolamo, 51
Second World War, 62, 89, 96, 112, 115
Siberia, 23, 58, 77, 135
Slavism, 63, 146
South America, 150
Soviets, formation of, 30-31
Spain, 47, 53
Stalin, Joseph, 94-109, 99*, 111-114, 116-117, 123-128, 124*-125*, 130-133, 135-137
Supreme Soviet, 30-31, 100
Switzerland, 22-23, 27

T

Trotsky, Leon, 57-63, 60*-61*, 69, 72, 83, 95, 100-105, 104*, 109, 126, 133-134
Tse-tung, Mao, 105
Turkey, 103

U

Ulyanov, 22-23
Union of Soviet Socialist Republics, 14, 73
United Nations, 128, 141

V

Versailles, 42

W

Washington, George, 82, 106
White Russians, 42-44, 59-62, 60*-61*, 70*-71*, 72, 75